D1766481

A

GUIDE TO TRACING YOUR ROSCOMMON ANCESTORS

John Hamrock

First published in 2007

Flyleaf Press
4 Spencer Villas
Glenageary
Co. Dublin, Ireland
www.flyleaf.ie

© 2007 John Hamrock

British Library cataloguing in Publications Data available

978-0-9539974-7-3

Cover Illustration:
Eoin Ryan

Layout:
Brian Smith

Dedication

To

My wife, Deirdre Breen
and my children
Aedán, Fergal and Marie-Chantal
also to my parents
James Stephen Hamrock and Mary Frances Walsh
and to all my family in America and Ireland

"And then there is the work! If the genealogical bug once bites you, you are a doomed man, and never again will you be happy except when attempting to trace the elusive ancestor. It has all the fascination of a game for one who loves it. It is like working out a chess problem or a cross-word puzzle, but much more exhilarating, for the pawns in this game were once human beings. You have ancestral charts in blank, which theoretically can be filled in completely with the names of your ancestors; and there is no elation akin to that which you experience when a long-sought forbear is discovered and an empty space on the chart becomes a name and a reality."[1]

Acknowledgements

I wish to express my gratitude for the valuable assistance provided to me by the staff of the following Irish and American repositories:

General Registrar's Office
National Archives and Records Administration, Regional Archives, Northeast Region, USA – Waltham, Massachusetts
New England Historic Genealogical Society Library
Representative Church Body Library
Roscommon County Library
Royal Irish Academy Library
The Gilbert Library, Dublin City Library
The National Library of Ireland
The National Archives of Ireland
The Registry of Deeds
University College Dublin Library
Valuation Office, Dublin

This book started out as an assignment for the National University of Ireland Certificate in Genealogy/Family History Course at the Adult Education Centre, UCD Dublin. I wish particularly to thank the course tutor, Sean Murphy, MA, for his guidance and encouragement throughout the course. I would also like to thank William Gacquin for providing valuable information on South Roscommon and Mike Lennon who revealed some family connections and who sparked my interest in Irish genealogy. I would also like to thank Eimear Lenahan for her documentation on the Lenahan family

Most importantly, I am thankful to my wife, Deirdre, and my children Aedán, Fergal, and Marie-Chantal for their patience and loving support. I also thank my parents, James Stephen Hamrock and Mary Frances Walsh Hamrock, for their love and support.

Table of Contents

	Abbreviations	8
Chapter 1.	Introduction	9
Chapter 2.	Conducting Family Research	13
Chapter 3.	Administrative Divisions	15
Chapter 4.	Civil Registration	23
Chapter 5.	Census and Census Substitutes	27
Chapter 6.	Church Records	35
Chapter 7.	Land Records	49
Chapter 8.	Estate Records	55
Chapter 9.	Grave Records and Inscriptions	79
Chapter 10.	Wills, Administrations and Marriage Records	83
Chapter 11.	Directories and Occupational Sources	91
Chapter 12.	Newspapers	95
Chapter 13.	Educational Records	99
Chapter 14.	Gaelic Genealogies	103
Chapter 15.	Surnames and Family Histories	107
Chapter 16.	Miscellaneous Sources	134
Chapter 17.	Further Reading	136
Chapter 18.	Useful Information	141
	Endnotes	146
	Index	148

Abbreviations

BIVRI	British Isles Vital Records Index (LDS CD-ROM set)
BL	British Library
BMD	Births, marriages and deaths
c.	circa (around)
Co.	County
C of I	Church of Ireland
DED	District Electoral Division
Ed.	Edited
EGFHS	East Galway Family History Society Ltd.
FAS	Foras Áiseanna Saothair, Ireland's National Training and Employment Authority
GO	Genealogical Office
GRO	General Register Office
IA	The Irish Ancestor magazine
IFHF	Irish Family History Foundation
IGI	International Genealogical Index
IGRS	Irish Genealogical Research Society
IMC	Irish Manuscripts Commission
Inc.	including
JRSAI	Journal of the Royal Society of Antiquities of Ireland
LC	Local Custody
LDS	Church of Jesus Christ of Latter Day Saints Family History Library
Ms(s)	manuscript(s)
NA	National Archives
NAI	National Archives of Ireland
n.d.	no date
NEHGS	New England Historic Genealogical Society
NLI	National Library of Ireland
NUI	National University of Ireland
PLU	Poor Law Union
Pos.	Positive
PRO	Public Record Office
PRONI	Public Record Office of Northern Ireland
pub.	published/publisher
RC	Roman Catholic
RCBL	Representative Church Body Library
RCL	Roscommon County Library
re	relating to
RHGC	Roscommon Heritage and Genealogy Company
RHAS	Roscommon Historical and Archaeological Society
RIA	Royal Irish Academy
RSAI	Royal Society of Antiquarians in Ireland
SHGC	Sligo Heritage and Genealogical Centre
SLC	Family History Library, Salt Lake City (& branches)
TCD	Trinity College Dublin
UCD	University College Dublin

Chapter 1   Introduction

Roscommon is a landlocked county in the province of Connaught and is 60 miles from north to south and 40 miles from west to east. The landscape is mainly flat except for the Braulieve mountains at the North-eastern corner, and the Curlew mountains to the northwest. Lough Key and Lough Gara also form part of the northern boundaries with Leitrim and Sligo. It is bounded to the east by the Shannon river and lakes and by counties Longford, Westmeath, Offaly, and to the west by the river Suck and counties Galway and Mayo. It is primarily an agricultural county, with generally fertile soil.

In the decade of the Great Famine, from its peak population in 1841 of 253,591 inhabitants, the population dropped by over 30% to 174,492 due to death and emigration. The following table (from British Parliamentary Papers: *The Census of Ireland for the Year 1851*, Alexander Thom, Dublin) illustrates the decline in each Barony. This decline continued over the following century and the current population (2002) is almost 54,000 and slowly increasing once again

Roscommon people have historically been predominantly Roman Catholic. The 1861 Census[2] provided the first reliable figures of Church membership and showed that the Irish population was 77% Catholic. In comparison, the diocese of Elphin, which makes up a large chunk of Roscommon, was 96% Catholic.[3] The religious denominations are further detailed on page 35.

The purpose of this guide is to direct beginner and experienced researchers to information on Roscommon ancestors within the confusing range of sources that exist. Further information on some sources is in the end-notes (page 146) which are numbered within each chapter. A particular goal is to inform readers about manuscript sources, most of which cannot be accessed over the internet. To avail of these resources one must visit archives or retain a professional genealogist.

Summary by Baronies

Baronies	Population in 1841	Population in 1851	No. of Inhabited Houses in 1841	No. of Inhabited Houses in 1851
Athlone	51,927	36,128	9,135	6,507
Ballintober, South	19,370	10,282	3,367	1,805
Ballintober, North	26,369	17,476	4,429	2,780
Ballymoe	8,061	4,803	1,342	846
Boyle	40,129	28,954	6,879	4,628
Castlereagh	27,886	22,255	4,918	3,597
Frenchpark	28,859	21,220	5,169	3,759
Moycarn	7,496	6,518	1,330	1,080
Roscommon	43,494	26,856	7,518	4,524
Total	**253,591**	**174,492**	**44,087**	**29,526**

Ireland has fewer genealogical sources than some other countries, but records are usually available back to the early nineteenth century, and if one is lucky, even earlier. The earlier records are generally those of the well-to-do or the educated, or others whose political, military or ecclesiastical activities inspired specific reference.

This is an exciting time for genealogy in Ireland with public interest growing at a steady pace. This growth in interest is evidenced by magazines such as Irish Roots (www.iol.ie/~irishrts/); by the provision of better research facilities; and by the availability of training. University College Dublin (www.ucd.ie) now offers Certificate and Diploma courses in Genealogy/Family History of which the writer is a graduate. There has also been steady growth in Irish genealogical societies.

It is advised that researchers take the time to visit Roscommon and meet relatives, if possible, to learn as much as possible directly from family members and local people. In addition to conducting research in Dublin repositories, it is also rewarding to visit the Roscommon County Library as the library staff are very helpful and the repository for genealogical and local history sources is a comfortable setting in which to do research.

This guide will be also helpful in researching ancestors in the seven counties which border Roscommon. The writer's paternal grandparents lived in neighbouring Mayo and Sligo. His grandmother, Ellen Cryan, was from the townland of Seefin, barony of Coolavin in County Sligo. When she emigrated, the family noted that they were from Roscommon as the closest town to their farm was Boyle in County Roscommon. Likewise, the writer's grandfather, James Hamrock, was from a small farm in the townland of Leow, near Ballyhaunis in Co. Mayo. They probably sold their produce and livestock in Ballinlough in Co. Roscommon as it was just as easy for the family to walk to market there as to walk to Ballyhaunis in Mayo.

The writer, John Hamrock, conducts research on Roscommon families and on families across the entire island of Ireland. He can be contacted at 19 Balally Avenue, Dundrum, Dublin 16, Ireland or by email at john. hamrock@yahoo.ie or visit his website www.ancestor.ie

It is not possible to cover every aspect of Roscommon genealogical research in this small guide. Almost certainly some items have been overlooked, and equally, new sources of genealogical relevance continue to be discovered. Nevetherless, it is hoped that the ideas or information in this book will enable a successful search for an elusive Roscommon ancestor.

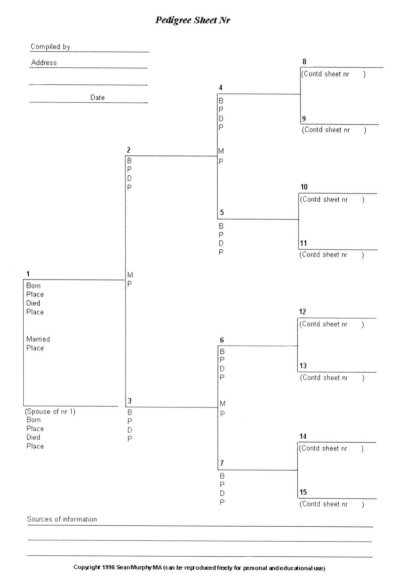

Pedigree Sheet Nr

Compiled by _____

Address _____

_____
Date _____

1
Born
Place
Died
Place

Married
Place

(Spouse of nr 1)
Born
Place
Died
Place

2
B
P
D
P

3
B
P
D
P

4
B
P
D
P

5
B
P
D
P

6
B
P
D
P

7
B
P
D
P

M
P

M
P

M
P

M
P

8
(Contd sheet nr   )

9
(Contd sheet nr   )

10
(Contd sheet nr   )

11
(Contd sheet nr   )

12
(Contd sheet nr   )

13
(Contd sheet nr   )

14
(Contd sheet nr   )

15
(Contd sheet nr   )

Sources of information _____

_____

_____

A typical pedigree chart used by family historians

Chapter 2   Conducting Family Research

A basic first step in family research is to obtain information from living relatives. Seek out older relatives and listen to their recollections of their relatives. Be warned however, not to become over-reliant on such recollections. Oral history can be misleading. It is best to try to anchor these stories with documented fact. Trace your ancestry from what is known to the unknown by using documented facts as your guide. The records which are usually used to do this are birth, death and marriage records. A fuller picture of an ancestor's life is established from building on factual information derived from using more than just one source.

To keep track of your information as it grows, it is important to prepare a family tree. This will both record the information and also when and where each piece of information was sourced. It is inevitable that you will need recheck some records at a later date. Several styles of sheets are available to organise your data, including circular charts, horizontal and vertical pedigree sheets. A sample of the horizontal pedigree sheet, which is a favourite, can be seen opposite and on http://homepage. eircom.net/~seanmurphy/dir/index.htm. Whichever system is used, accurately and copiously recording source information (a) helps the researcher to pick up where one has left off without having to redo research work; and (b) allows other family members to pick up and continue the research work.

An early step in the research process is to consult sources on the origins of the family name. These may give an indication of family history and locations, but rarely anything of specific relevance to your own family history. Some standard references by MacLysaght and Woulfe are described in Chapter 14.

Finally it is useful to understand the social history of the time and the place where one's ancestors lived. This will allow the researcher to better understand the environment and the social, economic and occupational challenges which their ancestors encountered during their lifetimes and which may have caused the creation of records which family researchers can utilise.

MOORE, a parish, in the half-barony of MOYCAR-NON, county of ROSCOMMON, and province of CON-NAUGHT, 2½ miles (E.) from Ballinasloe, on the road to Athlone, and on the rivers Shannon and Suck; containing 4376 inhabitants. Disturbances have occasionally occurred of late years at this place, which has been the scene of many outrages. The parish comprises 9856½ statute acres, chiefly arable and poor land; there are about 100 acres of bog, easily reclaimable, as there is a fall into the Shannon and Suck, which latter river merges into the Shannon, at right angles, at Shannon bridge · good limestone is abundant. Petty sessions are held at Ballydangan every Thursday; and there is a constabulary police station, about a mile from which, at Tully House, is a chief station of the constabulary force. The principal seats are Clonburn, the residence of J. Knight, Esq.; Falta, of T. Power, Esq.; Thomastown Park, of E. H. Naghten, Esq.; Castle Park, of W. Kelly, Esq.; Birch Grove, of Mrs. O'Shaughnessy; Killawn, of E. Duffy, Esq.; Tully, of Mr. Lowry, the chief constable; Woodpark, of Owen Lynch, Esq.; Kilbegley, of B. Newcomen, Esq.; Correen, of J. T. Potts, Esq.; two at Shannon Bridge, the respective residences of A. and D. Lynch, Esqrs.; and Dromalga Cottage, the property of Sir R. St. George, Bart., now occupied by Mr. Dexter. The living is a rectory and vicarage, in the diocese of Tuam, episcopally united to the vicarage of Drum, and in the patronage of the Bishop : the tithes amount to £224. 10., of which £12 is payable to the dean of Clonfert; and the gross tithes of the benefice are £302. 10. The church is a neat building, erected, in 1825, by a gift of £900 from the late Board of First Fruits : the basement story is appropriated as a residence for the sexton's family. The R. C. parish is co-extensive with that of the Established Church, and contains a chapel at Clonfad and another at Moore. There are two private schools, in which are about 100 children. At Clonburn, Moore, and Kilbegley, are ruins of churches with burial-grounds attached.

A description of the civil parish of Moore from the 'Topographical Dictionary of Ireland by Samuel Lewis (1837)

Chapter 3   Administrative Divisions

An ancestor's address is an essential part of their identity. It is therefore important to understand the composition of addresses as they are cited. All Irish counties were divided into different areas or divisions for civil or Church (Ecclesiastical) administration purposes. The major Civil and Ecclesiastical divisions in Roscommon are discussed below:

Civil Divisions: Civil divisions were established for administration of land ownership and local government. They range from the largest, the province, to the smallest, which is the townland.

Province: Roscommon is in the province of Connaught or Connacht. Provinces are based on five ancient Irish kingdoms, the other four being Leinster, Meath, Munster and Ulster. Meath was later merged with Leinster to create the current four provinces.

County: A county is a significant administrative unit and many records are organised at county level. The borders of Roscommon were formed in 1565 (see p.18). Note that some townlands and parishes straddle the county border. Some of these border areas have also been 'moved' e.g. the Local Government (Ireland) Act, 1898 transferred several townlands from Mayo and Galway to Roscommon.[4]

Barony: Baronies and half baronies are sub-units of counties. The barony is not used much after the 18th century. They are Boyle, Frenchpark, Castlereagh, Roscommon, Ballintober North & South, Ballymoe, Athlone, and Moycarn (see map P.18)

Civil Parish: Civil parishes are a very important division for most records. They should not be confused with "ecclesiastical parishes" which are territories administered by Irish churches.

Townland: The townland is the smallest unit of land division and is very important in finding the specific location of a family. In general they contain a few hundred acres of land, but can vary from 10 acres to several thousand.

Poor Law Union (PLU): Poor Law Unions were areas within which taxes were collected to alleviate the plight of the poor, and to maintain workhouses. Usually centered on a market town, they include an area of fifteen mile radius. Later on, the PLU became the area in which civil births, marriages and deaths were registered.

Electoral Divisions: Poor Law Unions were later sub-divided into District Electoral Divisions **(DEDs)** for the purposes of voter registration and other administration.

Ecclesiastical Divisions: The church maintained a separate system of administration, which is also based on ancient land areas. There are overlaps, but they are effectively separate. They are important not only for records such as baptisms and marriages, but also because the Church of Ireland was responsible for administration of wills and other records for a long period of Irish history.

Diocese: The diocese is the area under the authority of a bishop. Their boundaries have remained relatively unchanged since the twelfth century and (with minor variations) are used by both the Church of Ireland and the Roman Catholic Church. Roscommon is within the dioceses of Achrony, Ardagh, Clonfert, Elphin, and Tuam

Church of Ireland Parish. These are identical to civil parishes – see map p.18

Roman Catholic Parish. These are sometimes equivalent to a civil parish, but usually not. Theie size has evolved over history to cater for changing population sizes and other factors.

Probate Districts: Following the removal of civil duties from the Church of Ireland in 1858, a civil infrastructure was established for Probate administration. The divisions used for proving wills and for granting administrations include a Principal Registry and District Registries. Roscommon was served by the District Registry of Tuam.

Some Guides on Administrative Divisions:

Alphabetical Index to Townlands & Towns, Parishes & Baronies of Ireland (1851)
Commonly known as the 1851 Townland Index, this is a comprehensive index. It was originally published by Thoms (Dublin) and republished by Genealogical Publishing Co. (Baltimore). It is a standard reference in libraries with Irish interest holdings.

General Topographical Index to Townlands and Towns of Ireland (1901): This index is similar to the 1851 Index, but also lists the relevant District Electoral Divisions which are important when accessing certain land records. (see Chapter 7)

Topographical Dictionary of Ireland by Samuel Lewis (Dublin 1837). This useful guide contains a brief history and summary of economic and social conditions in all parishes and towns, and a map. It also lists major local landowners of the day. It has been republished and digitized in many different forms and is widely available. (see p.14)

Parliamentary Gazetteer of Ireland (1844/5). This is similar to Lewis's *Topographical Dictionary of Ireland* in content. It is available in many libraries.

Ordnance Survey Field Name Books: These notebooks were compiled by the surveyors who drew the first official maps during the nineteenth century (see www.ordnancesurvey.ie). Information includes townland names, location and landowners' names. The original manuscripts are on microfilm at the NLI and hardcopy typescripts are also available.

Townlands in Poor Law Unions. Higginson, (Salem, Mass.) 1997 by George Handran is a useful reference as it will identify adjacent townlands within a civil parish or Poor Law Union.

Civil Parishes of County Roscommon

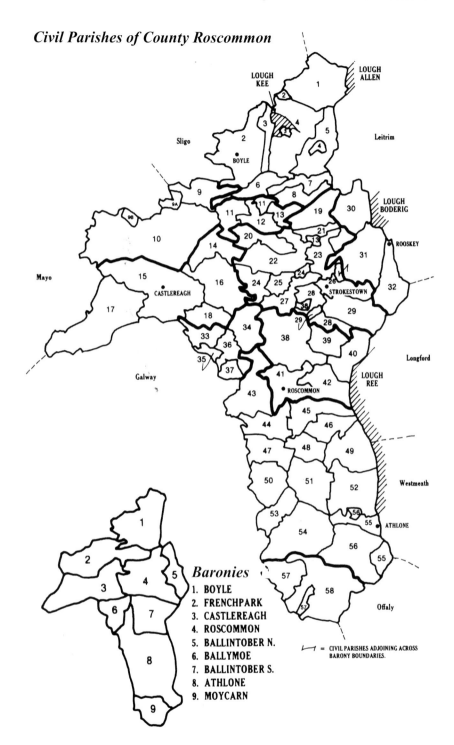

Baronies
1. BOYLE
2. FRENCHPARK
3. CASTLEREAGH
4. ROSCOMMON
5. BALLINTOBER N.
6. BALLYMOE
7. BALLINTOBER S.
8. ATHLONE
9. MOYCARN

⌐ = CIVIL PARISHES ADJOINING ACROSS BARONY BOUNDARIES.

Roscommon Civil Parishes
as Numbered on Map

1. Kilronan	29. Lissonuffy
2. Boyle	30. Kilmore
3. Kilbryan	31. Kilglass
4. Ardcarn	32. Termonbarry
5. Tumna	33. Drumatemple
6. Eastersnow or Estersnow	34. Cloonygormican
7. Killukin (see also 27)	35. Ballynakill
8. Killumod	36. Oran
9. Kilnamanagh	37. Dunamon
9a. Kilcolman	38. Kilbride
9b. Castlemore	39. Kilgefin
10. Tibohine	40. Cloontuskert
11. Kilcolagh	41. Roscommon
12. Kilmacumsy	42. Kilteevan
13. Creeve	43. Fuerty
14. Kilcorkey	44. Athleague
15. Kilkeevan	45. Kilmeane
16. Baslick	46. Killinvoy or Killenvoy
17. Kiltullagh	47. Tisrara
18. Ballintober	48. Rahara
19. Aughrim	49. St. John's or Ivernoon
20. Shankill	50. Taghboy
21. Clooncraff	51. Cam or Camma
22. Elphin	52. Kiltoom
23. Kiltrustan	53. Dysart or Dysert
24. Ogulla	54.Taghmaconnell or Taughmaconnell
25. Kilcooly	55. St. Peter's
26. Bumlin	56. Drum
27. Killukin (See also 7)	57. Creagh
28. Cloonfinlough	58. Moore

Roscommon Civil Parishes
in Alphabetical Order

Ardcarn: 4	Kilglass: 31
Athleague: 44	Kelkeevan: 15
Aughrim: 19	Killinvoy of Killenvoy: 46
Ballintober: 18	Killukin (1): 7
Ballynakill: 35	Killukin (2): 27
Baslick: 16	Killumod: 8
Boyle: 2	Kilmacumsy: 12
Bumlin: 26	Kilmeane: 45
Cam or Camma: 51	Kilmore: 30
Castlemore: 9b	Kilnamanagh: 9
Clooncraff: 21	Kilronan: 1
Cloonfinlough: 28	Kilteevan: 42
Cloontuskert: 40	Kiltoom: 52
Cloonygormican: 34	Kiltrustan: 23
Creagh: 57	Kiltullagh: 17
Creeve: 13	Lissonuffy: 29
Drum: 56	Moore: 58
Drumtemple: 33	Ogulla: 24
Dunamon: 37	Oran: 36
Dysart or Dysert: 53	Rahara: 48
Eastersnow or Estersnow: 6	Roscommon: 41
Elphin: 22	Shankill: 20
Fuerty: 43	St. John's or Ivernoon: 49
Kilbride: 38	St. Peter's: 55
Kilbryan: 3	Taghboy: 50
Kilcolagh: 12	Taghmaconnell or Taughmaconell: 54
Kilcolman: 9a	Termonbarry: 32
Kilcooly: 25	Tibohine: 10
Kilcorkey: 14	Tisrara: 47
Kilgefin: 39	Tumna: 5

Irish Historic Maps

The Ordnance Survey Ireland website (www.irishhistoricmaps.ie) contains 30,000 visual images of maps in State and University archives. Most of these span two eras, from 1824 to 1847, and from 1888 to 1913. Many are detailed and show locations of buildings, farms and streets, and other rich details about 19th century life: individual plots of land, cemeteries, schools, hospitals, businesses, factories, wells, and even trees and bushes. If the necessary information is available, the locations of individual dwellings may be found and local details may help provide information about the life they might have led.

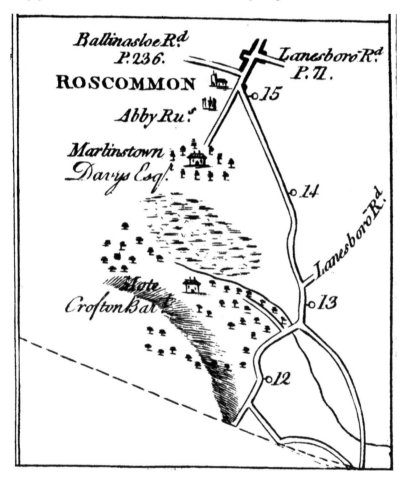

Map of area around Roscommon town from Taylor & Skinner
'Maps of the Roads of Ireland' (1778) – republished 1969
by Irish University Press (Shannon).

Superintendent Registrar's District __Athlone__   Registrar's District __Bridestrete__

1864. DEATHS Registered in the District of __Bridewele__ in the Union of __Athlone__ in the County of __Roscommon__

No.	Date and Place of Death.	Name and Surname.	Sex.	Condition.	Age last Birthday.	Rank, Profession, or Occupation.	Certified Cause of Death, and Duration of Illness.	Signature, Qualification, and Residence of Informant.	When Registered.	Signature of Registrar.
26	Third April 2nd 1864 Littletane	Jonathan Hamrock	Male	Married Widower	94 years	Landholder	Old age	Henry Hamrock Nephew of Decd. Who was in house at Death Bridewele	Fifth April 23rd 1864	John Kilbait

Copy of death record from GRO register giving the details of Jonathan Hamrock's death.

Chapter 4   Civil Registration

A valuable source of family information is civil records of births, marriages and deaths. Civil registrations in Ireland commenced in 1845 with non-Catholic marriages. Registration for all births, marriages, and deaths only began in 1864. The following records are available:

Births: (from 1864). These specify the child's name; date and place of birth; name and occupation of father; name and maiden name of mother; and name of the informant (the person registering the birth).

Marriages: (Non-Catholic marriages from 1845; all marriages from 1864). These specify place and date of marriage; names, ages, address and occupations of groom and bride; the name and occupation of the fathers of groom and bride; and the witnesses.

Deaths: (from 1864). These specify date and place of death; the name of the person who died; marital status, age, occupation; the cause of death; and details of the informant.

These records are the responsibility of the General Register Office (GRO) which has recently been relocated from Dublin to Roscommon as part of a programme of decentralization of Government offices. Copies of certificates are still available at the Dublin office (see Chapter 18) where there is also a search room. A full list of contact points is available on the GRO website at www.groireland.ie.

Indexes to all the registers from 1845 can be accessed in the Search Room of the GRO in Dublin, and those for the District of Roscommon can be accessed at the Local office in Roscommon (see p. 146). The registers themselves cannot be inspected, but copies of each entry can be purchased. Payment is required to access the records and researchers should therefore be well organized with their search information before conducting an on site GRO search. One can also write to the GRO to request a search, but only within a specific search period of 5 years and only for a specific event (i.e. they will not list all persons with a particular name). A professional researcher must be hired to do this.

The indexes are in alphabetical order by surname. The death index also notes the age at death which is useful in locating the correct person. Registration was recorded within Registration Districts, which correspond to the Poor Law Unions (see p.16). If you have an address for your family, you should therefore establish the Registration District in which it is located in advance of a visit to the GRO.

The researcher should be aware that the indexes are based on the date of registration of the event, and not the date on which it occurred. As registration was dependent on family members, it could take weeks, months or longer before an event was registered. Late registrations can be located at the back of the related yearly index or in one of the following periods. In addition, particularly in the early years of the civil registration process, many events were not registered at all.

Access to GRO Records
The indexes of the GRO Records can be consulted in the following archives. Contact details for each are in Chapter 18.

Church of Jesus Christ of Latter Day Saints (LDS): LDS have compiled the International Genealogical Index (IGI) which includes civil registration details. The LDS microfilms of births marriage and death records are available in the LDS Library and a copy is in the General Register Office. Information can be obtained on their website www.familysearch.org/. Family Search issued in 2001 a collection of CD-ROMs called the *British Isles Vital Records Index for England, Ireland Scotland and Wales*. Compared to other Irish counties in this collection, which is by no means complete, a sizeable number of Roscommon births and christenings (107, 519 entries) and Marriages (12,730 entries) are recorded.

Dublin City Library: This library has branch status of the LDS Library and has the IGI microfilm copies of the LDS civil registration indexes of births, marriages, and deaths. It is often easier to obtain information on the civil registration microfilm indexes and then go to the GRO to purchase copies rather than working in the often overcrowded GRO research room.

National Library of Ireland (NLI): holds an index to births in 1864, 1865, and 1866. (Ref: LB Thom 3121). It also holds an index of deceased Irish Seamen from 1887 to 1949.

Some useful tips on finding in GRO records are:

Spelling. Check all variations of name spelling e.g. Mahony, Mahoney, O'Mahoney etc. The MacLysaght and other guides (see p 103) will provide the common variations.

Un-named Children: Christian names may not have been decided at the time of registration, in which case the child will be registered as Female or Male. Check for male or female entries which are the final entries under a particular surname.

Checking Marriages: Marriages are indexed under both bride and groom surnames. Therefore, if you are searching a very common name (e.g. Mary Kelly) and want to ensure that a particular entry is 'your' Mary, you can check under the groom's name. If it has the same reference numbers, it is almost certainly the same marriage.

18	Henry Dillon in Keile and Shanballyloske. . .. Turlogh oge mc Dowell here	Gallagmaghery ½ a qr. Cont. of Arrable Land .. *r.* 1 : Cart. : 1 ; Cart.
19	Hugh oge ó Connor in Eden .. .. In Garryduffe in Gollogh-maghry	Galloghmaghry ye other ½ Quart. containing of Arrable Land .. 1 Cart : 1 Cart : /In Magalla : 8 qrs.
20	Xtopher Delahide .. Thomas Dillon	Carrowbane : 1 qr. containing of arrable .. .. .. ½ gn : ½ gn :
21	Tumultogh Boy hanly ..	—*ibm*— Two gneeves of Carrowbane Cont. of arrable Land .. .. more of Pasturable Wood ..
22	Wony Connor Widd .. Richard ffarrolls Land ..	: *ibm* : Three gneeves of Carrowbane con-taining of arab Land .. more a claime as part of ye Same out of Cloneashellmore Cont. of arrable & Pasture .. ..
23	Dwaltagh mc : Bryen Hanley	Coolegarry 4 gneeves Cont. of arrable & Pasture .. ..
24 & 25		Feaghmore & ⎫ ⎬2 gneeves .. Feaghbegg ⎭ of arrable & Pasture .. ..
	Gillernow mc : Dermott Hanly .. Hugh Oge Connor of ffeaghbegg ..	½ a gneeve 1 Cartron
26	Rory mc : Ballow mc : Teige Hanley ». ..	Carrow Imuchan : 1 qr. Curragh 2 gneeves Cont. of Arrable & Pasture .. ..
	Gillernow mc : Dermot Hanly in Carrow Ivulchan	1 gneeve

A page from the 'Books of Survey and Distribution 1654-1656' published by the Irish Manuscripts Commission 1949

Chapter 5   Census and Census Substitutes

A census of population was taken every 10 years since 1821, but the original household returns survive only for the 1901 and 1911 censuses. Those for other years were destroyed either by government order or in the PRO Fire. There are some returns for 1821, 1831, 1841 and 1851, but only a very small number concern Roscommon. However, there are other specialist and local censuses taken over the centuries for a range of reasons. These very useful sources are listed below by date.

1585; The Compossicion Booke of Connought, (IMC, Dublin, 1936). Details (including property holdings) of an agreement with the Gaelic Chiefs of Connaught and County Clare for a resettlement of that area under feudal plan.

1630 – 39: Particulars of quarters of lands in each barony within …. Roscommon and …Mayo. A book of every man's particular estate in the barony of Clan-William, (c. 1630-39). London: British Museum: Harleian Ms. 2048: (Extracts) NLI n.1674 p.1416.

1654-56: Books of Survey and Distribution. As a result of the Cromwellian land settlement of the 1650s, lands were confiscated from those involved in the rebellion of 1641 and distributed to new owners (Protestant, usually English and some Huguenots). These were mainly adventurers, who had financed Cromwell's army, and his soldiers, who received land in lieu of pay. Following the restoration of Charles II, this settlement was modified by the Acts of Settlement (1662) and Explanation (1665). These Books show ownership of land as recorded in the various surveys between 1636 and 1660, but does not generally identify tenants and under-tenants (see p.26). Originals are in the NAI and PRONI. Vol I. R.C. Simington, Dublin: Stationery Office, 1949. SLC film 96524.

THE CENSUS OF ELPHIN 1749

Com~Roscomon Parish of	Place of Abode	Names and Religion	Proffession	Children under 14 Prot.	Children under 14 Paps.	Children above 14 Prot.	Children above 14 Paps.	Men Servts Prot.	Men Servts Paps.	Women Servts Prot.	Women Servts Paps.
[f.286]Killukin	Doon	Mary Cooper widow Prot	Farmer	5		.			1		2
		Patk. Meahan & wife Pap	Servant		2				1		2
		John Bern & wife Pap	Herd		1						1
		Fran. Bern & wife Pap	Labourer		2						
		Thady Durneen & wife Pap	Pumpmaker		3				1		
		Thos. Griskin & wife Pap	Labourer		3						
		John Kennedy & wife Pap	Labourer		1						1
		Sus. Cummin widow Pap	Cottier		1		4				
		Michl. Burk & wife Pap	Labourer		4				1		
	Rathmore	John Flanigan Pap	Labourer		1		3				1
		Geo. Coyl & wife Pap	Labourer		3						
		Michl. Brenan & wife Pap	Mercht.		4				1		2
		Patk. Rowen & wife Pap	Labourer		1						1
		Willm. Higgins & wife Pap	Labourer		3		1				
		John O Hara & wife Pap	Labourer		2				1		
		Patk. Smith & wife Pap	Labourer		3						1

Extract from 'The Census of Elphin 1749'
Published by the Irish Manuscripts Commission (2005)

1654-58: The Transplantation to Connacht (R.C. Simington, Irish University Press for IMC (1970). The occupants of lands confiscated by Cromwell (see 1654-56) were transplanted to the West, including Roscommon. For instance, the baronies of Athlone and Moycarn were assigned to 'Inhabitants of Counties Cork and Wexford' and Ballintober, Ballymoe, Boyle and Roscommon were assigned to 'Inhabitants of the Counties of Kildare, Meath, Queen's (Laoighs)[sic] and Dublin.

1659*:* **The Census of Ireland circa 1659** was compiled by Sir William Petty, who was responsible for the Civil Survey. This compilation was edited by Séamus Pender ("Pender's Census") and published by the Dublin Stationery Office in 1939 (NLI I 6551, SLC film 924648). It gives the names of the titulados, (those with title to land) and the total number of persons (English and Irish) resident on each townland. It is only useful for sizeable landlords, but also lists the "Principall [sic] Irish Names and their Number" in each barony.

1690-1900: **Records of Athlone and District (1690-1900)**. Four volumes of handwritten stories on people and places in Roscommon. Many seem to be transcribed from newspapers, but there are other lists such as 'Reward for Sheriffs Polling Books,' 'Persons whose cattle was houghed in Co. Rosc.,' etc. Compiled by Malachy Moran. NLI Ms. 1547 – 1550, formerly GO 674-678; and SLC films 100214-6.

1691: **Irish Jacobites** [Lists from T.C.D. Ms. N.1.3], *Analecta Hibernica*, No. 22, IMC 1960. A list of men outlawed for treason against William III. Provides name, location etc, e.g. 'Terrence M'Dermott, Ballintobber, kt; Miles M'Dermott, Corraghsallagh, gent; Thomas Plunkett, Ardkenagh, gent, son of Richard'.

1704-1839: The Convert Rolls. Roman Catholics who converted to the Church of Ireland during the Penal Times. It lists the name, date of conversion and (for about half) address and other information. Published in several works. The Convert Rolls Eileen O'Byrne, IMC Dublin, 1981 and also O'Byrne, E., editor, *The Convert Rolls*; *The Calendar of the Convert Rolls, 1703-1838*; Chamney, Anne, editor, *Fr. Wallace Clare's Annotated List of Converts, 1703-78*, IMC Dublin, 2005. This edition is in two parts. Part one provides a list of 5,780 *names,* Fr. Wallace Clare's list contains 1,207 names. (see p.30).

174   CONVERT ROLLS

McDermott, Barnaby, and Alice, his wife, of Bumlin, cert. 30 May 1761, enrolled 6 June 1761 (A). McDermot, Barnaby, of Strokestown, d. Elphin, taylor, and Alice, his wife, conformity 22 February 1761 (B). (D).

McDermott, Bryan, Elphin, cert. 17 May 1735, enrolled 2 June 1735 (A). D. Elphin, conformity 11 February 1734 (B). Of Strokestown, Co Roscommon, gent. (D).

McDermott, Edmond, cert. 12 October 1771, enrolled 24 October 1771 (A). Late of Emlagh, Co Roscommon, now of Dublin, conformity 12 October 1771 (B). (D).

McDermott, Edward, Esq., Dublin, cert. 15 May 1763, enrolled 20 May 1763 (A). Now of St Bridget's parish, conformity 14 May 1763 (B).

McDermott, Edward, Esq., cert. 22 December 1763, enrolled 23 March 1764 (A). Now of Dublin, conformity 20 December 1763 (B). (D).

McDermott, John, of Lusk, cert. and enrolled 28 December 1749 (A). D. Dublin, conformity 24 December 1749 (B). Gent. (D).

McDermott, John. See McDermott, Ann.

McDermott, Mary, cert. 17 February 1752, enrolled 27 February 1752 (A). Now of Dublin, conformity 14 February 1752 (B).

McDermott, Mary, cert. 15 December 1763, enrolled 10 January 1764 (A). McDermott, Mrs Mary, now of Dublin, conformity 11 December 1763 (D). (D).

Abstract from the 'Convert Rolls' by Eileen O'Byrne (IMC) 1981

1746-1772: **Army Lists** for Athlone and elsewhere. GO Ms 579.

1749: The Census of Elphin. Compiled to determine the number of Protestants and Roman Catholics in Elphin diocese. It lists the householders in each town and townland; occupations; and numbers and sex of children and servants.[5] The original is in the NAI (1A 36 13), NAI MFS 6, NAI M 2466; SLC film 101781; NLI n. 542 p. 923. See also *The Census of Elphin 1749*, ed. Marie-Louise Legg with a statistical analysis by Brian Gurrin. IMC 2005-see p.28. (www. irishmanuscripts.ie), The data is also accessible in electronic form, by subscription, at www.irishorigins.com.

1760-86: **Rental of Boswell Estate**, Kilronan parish, NLI p.4937 (major tenants only)

1761: **Militia List** for Co. Roscommon, etc. GO Ms. 680.

1778: **Rental of the Crofton Estate**. Nine parishes. NLI Ms. 19672

1780: Freeholders in Co. Roscommon. GO Ms. 442. Also SLC film 100181

1783: **Poll Book** i.e. list of registered electors for parliamentary election. Aug. 25-29, 1783; NLI Ms. 3086

1790-1799: **Several Lists of Freeholders** C. 30 lists. NLI Ms. 10130

1792: **Rentals of the Gunning Estate**; NLI Ms. 10152 (major tenants only in the civil parishes of Athleague, Fuerty, and Kilcooley).

1792 and 1804: **Rentals of Dundas Estate**; NLI Ms. 2787 (major tenants only in the civil parishes of Boyle, Estersnow, Kilnamanagh, and Tumna).

1796: **Spinning Wheel Premium List**: List of 3,000 Roscommon individuals who received awards for planting flax: full name, and civil parish in which the flax was grown. NLI ir 633411117; NAI and on CD from Family Tree Maker.

1796: List of officers and men in the Loughglin cavalry. Oxford: County Record Office: Ms. Dil. XXII, C. 2: Dillon Papers: n. 5208 p. 5312.

1798: The 1798 Rebellion: Claimants and Surrenders, ed. Ian Cantwell, CD-ROM Eneclann (2005). Lists rebels and those whose property was damaged. There are 15 Roscommon claimants.

1801-1806: **Rentals on Clonbrock Estate**; Taughmaconnell Parish; NLI Ms. 19501

1813-21: Registers of Freeholders (alphabetically arranged within each barony; gives names, addresses, location of freehold, etc.). NLI ILB 324

1821: **NAI Thrift Abstracts**: Falley refers to information on various families copied from the 1821 Census [NAI, Dublin, 58th Report, p. 33]).[6]

1823-1838 Tithe Applotment Survey (see Chapter 7 Land Records).

CENSUS OF IRELAND, 1901.

(Two Examples of the mode of filling up this Table are given on the other side.)

FORM A.

No. on Form B.

RETURN of the MEMBERS of this FAMILY and their VISITORS, BOARDERS, SERVANTS, &c., who slept or abode in this House on the night of SUNDAY, the 31st of MARCH, 1901.

NAME and SURNAME	RELATION to Head of Family	RELIGIOUS PROFESSION	EDUCATION	AGE		SEX		RANK, PROFESSION, or OCCUPATION	MARRIAGE	WHERE BORN	IRISH LANGUAGE	If Deaf and Dumb; Dumb only; Blind; Imbecile or Idiot; or Lunatic
Christian	Surname				Years	Months	M	F					
Patrick	Lenehan	Head of Family	Roman Catholic	Read & write	40		M		Farmer	Married	Co. Roscommon	✓	✓
Ellen	Lenehan	Wife	Roman Catholic	Read and Write	33			F	Farmers Wife	Married	Co Roscommon	✓	✓
John	Lenehan	Son	Roman Catholic	Read and Write	10		M		Scholar	Not Married	Co Roscommon	✓	✓
Michael	Lenehan	Son	Roman Catholic	Read	8		M		Scholar		Co Roscommon	✓	✓
James	Lenehan	Son	Roman Catholic	✓	4		M		Scholar		Co Roscommon	✓	✓
Aggnes	Lenehan	Daughter	Roman Catholic	✓	3			F			Co Roscommon	✓	✓
Thomas	Lenehan	Son	Roman Catholic	✓	2		M				Co Roscommon	✓	✓
James	Lenehan	Son	Roman Catholic			3	M				Co Roscommon		✓

I hereby certify, as required by the Act 63 Vic., cap. 6, s. 6 (1), that the foregoing Return is correct, according to the best of my knowledge and belief

(Signature of Enumerator.)

I believe the foregoing to be a true Return.

(Signature of Head of Family).

1901 Census of Ireland return, the details of which were recorded on the 31st March 1901

1830-47: Detailed account of **Ballykilcline townland**, Kilglass parish. See 1847.

1833: **Rental of the Crofton Estate**; Tumna parish; NLI Ms. 4531.

1834: **Tenants Listing in Moore Parish**. NLI Ms. 24880.

1836-1840: **Tenants on the Tenison Estate**; Ardcarn and Kilronan; NLI Ms. 5101.

1836-44: **List of Qualified Voters** (by barony; gives address). NLI Ir. 32341 R 20.

1836-1861: **Deed Extracts** (Athlone 1836-61; Roscommon 1720-1828). Longford/Westmeath Library (Burgess Papers); SLC film 1279274.

1837: **Marksmen** (i.e. illiterate voters) Athlone Borough *Parliamentary Papers 1837*, Reports from Committees, Vol. II (1), Appendix A

1839: **Person who obtained Game Certificates** in Roscommon, etc. PRONI T 688.

1841: **Some extracts**. NAI Thrift Abstracts

1843: **Workhouse records** of Carrick-on-Shannon union 1843-82. Leitrim Co. Library

1843: **Voters List** for Roscommon. NAI 1843/59.

1847-48: **Tenants From Ballykilcline** (Kilglass parish) who Emigrated Under State-aided Scheme. (names, ages, and relationships of 336 people, and shipping dates). In Eilish Ellis, *Emigrants from Ireland 1847-52*. Baltimore: Genealogical Publishing Co., 1977, pp. 10-21. Analecta Hibernica, No. 22, 1960. Includes a listing of evictions around 1850 from the Pakenham-Mahon Estate. The listing is more detailed, (in some respects) than the 1901 Census. (See p 27)

1848: **Male Catholic inhabitants of the parish of Boyle**. NLI Pos 4692

1851: Some extracts from the Thrift Abstracts in the NAI (NAI). Copies of census returns relating to the family of Cregg. (NAI M. 5249 (12)): Gearty family (M. 5249 (28)): & Kelly (NAI M 5249 (34))

1853: Map of County.. from documents of Poor Law Boundary Commissions. Alphabetical list of 251 proprietors, 1853. NLI 21 F. 103 (8).

1857 – 1858: Griffith's Valuation. See Chapter 7 - Land Records

1861: Athlone voters. Westmeath County Library. Also LDS film 1279285

1865-98: **Athlone Loan Society Accounts**. Longford/Westmeath Library and SLC films 1279277-81.

1901: **Government Census**. Census of 31st March, 1901 for every household. The details for every resident are Name; Relationship to Head of Family; Religion; Literacy; Age; Sex; Occupation; Marital Status; Birthplace; Ability to speak Irish, and Infirmities. Originals are in the NAI; copies are at SLC films 850470-85, 851571-81. On-line full indexes of this census are on a searchable data-base at www. leitrim-roscommon.com.

1908: **Pension Claim Forms**. In 1908 old age pensions were introduced for those over 70 years of age. As civil registration of birth only began in 1864, some people used census information to prove their age. This was done by requesting an official search of the census returns of 1841 and 1851. The forms used for these searches, including hand-written notes on the results, are still extant in the NAI. Additionally there are some other copies made from the returns of 1821-51. There are 1,052 forms for Roscommon (reference Cen S/25/1-1052), most of which relate to 1841 and 1851.

1911: **Government Census**. Census of 2nd of April 1911. The details for each resident are: Name; Relationship to Head of Family; Religion; Literacy; Age; Occupation; Marital Status; Number of Years Married; Birthplace; Languages Spoken (i.e., Irish or English or both) and Infirmities. Additionally to the 1901 Census, it states for each married woman the number of children born and the number then living. Returns are held at the NAI.

Chapter 6   Church Records

Church records are a crucial source of information on baptisms, marriages and burials. To effectively use them, it is obviously important to know the religious denomination of your ancestor and, ideally, where they may have been baptized or married or buried. One useful reference guide on the records created by the different denominations is James Ryan (ed.) *Irish Church Records,* Flyleaf Press, Dublin, 2001.

The 1861 Census of Ireland provided the first reliable figures of Church membership. Of the total population of 5.75 million, 77 per cent were Catholics.[7] The sample in the table below for the diocese of Elphin, making up a large proportion of County Roscommon, shows the proportion of Catholics to be much greater than the country as a whole, representing about 94 per cent of the population of Elphin diocese.[8]

Religious denominations in Diocese of Elphin in 1861	
Catholic	189,568
Protestant	10,444
Presbyterian	903
Methodist	721
Quaker	2
Others	239
Total	201,877
% Catholic	93.9

Church of Ireland Records In 1861 about 5% of the population of Roscommon was Church of Ireland. Until 1869 this was the State Church and official recorder of marriages, baptisms and burials.

As civil recording of these events was introduced (see Chapter 4), these records were brought for 'safe-keeping' to the PRO where approximately 33% were destroyed in a fire in 1922. The lost records are indicated below as "Destroyed". Note, however, that Church of Ireland marriage records are available from 1845 onwards in the GRO. Most of the extant records are indexed by the Roscommon Heritage and Genealogical Society (see Chapter 18).

Baptismal records usually provide names of the child, father (full name) mother (first name) and officiating minister. Marriage records provide the names of bride and groom and clergyman. Vestry books, which record details of parish management, may be available for some areas. They include mention of individual parishioners in relation to local tithe collections, care of orphans, constabulary, etc.

Most Church of Ireland parish records are either held in the custody of the local parishes (LC = Local Custody) or at the Representative Church Body Library (RCBL - see Chapter 18). The *Church of Ireland Directory* provides contact information on parish clergymen.

The Church of Jesus Christ of Latter Day Saints has also microfilmed many Church of Ireland Records (contact details are also provided in Chapter 18.

The researcher can also consult the NAI Church of Ireland parish records catalogue available both at the NAI and NLI also the *Guide to Church Records: Public Record Office of Northern Ireland* (PRONI, 1994)

The table on the following pages show the parishes, the periods for which records are available (or destroyed) and their location. Diocese are indicated by AR (Ardagh) EL (Elphin); CL (Clonfert) and TU (Tuam).

Church of Ireland Records and Locations

Parish	Diocese	Baptisms	Marriages	Burials	Records Location
Ahanagh (see also Boyle)	EL	1856-1875			LC
Ardcarne	EL	1830-1842	1813-1904	1820-1841	RCBL, RHGC
Ardclare	EL	1880-1900	1860-1919		RCBL, RHGC
Athleague	EL	1876-1932	1846-1910	1879-1979	RCBL, RHGC
Athlone, St. Peter's					RCBL
	EL	1873-1941	1845-1941		RHGC (1845 only)
Aughrim	EL	1879-	1849-		LC, RHGC
Ballinlough	TU	1822-	1822-	1831-	LC, RHGC
Ballyforan	EL	1847-	1851-		LC, RHGC
Ballygar	EL	1880-			LC, RHGC
Battlebridge	(see Toomna)				
Boyle	EL	1793-1875	1793-1845	1793-1875	LC
Bumlin	EL	1811-1971	1811-1919	1811-1985	RCBL
Croghan	EL	1862-1876		1860-1876	

Parish					
Donamon	EL		1847-1945		RCBL
(see also Fuerty)					
Drum	CL	1800-1902			Destroyed
Eastersnow	EL		1803-1877	1808-1886	RCBL
Elphin	EL	1896-1955	1845-1944	1897-1951	RCBL
Fuerty	EL		1847-1873		RCBL
(see also Donamon)					
Kilbryan	EL	1852-1958	1857-1960		RCBL
Kilcorkey	EL				(No inventory)
Kilcoffin	EL		1845-1863		RCBL
(or Kilgeffin)					
Kilglass	EL	1882-?	1823-1880	1825-1848	RCBL
Kilkeevan	EL	1748-1994	1784-1962	1784-1937	RCBL
Killenvoy	EL	1878-2000	1847-1937	1879-1966	RCBL
Kilgeffin	EL		1845-1863		RCBL
Killukin	EL	1880-1900	1860-1919		RCBL
(see also Ardclare)					
Killumod	(see Aughrim)				
Kilmore	EL				Destroyed

Parish	AR				
Kilronan					Destroyed
Kiltoom *	EL	1797-1943	1802-1910	1801-1840	RCBL
Kiltullagh	TU	1822-1875	1822-1875	1822-1875	LC
Loughglinn	EL	1877-1954	1845-1938		RCBL
Moore & Drum	CL				Destroyed
Oran	EL	1885-1948	1845-1897		RCBL
Roscommon & Kilbride	EL		1845-1946		RCBL
St. John	(see Killenvoy)				
St. Peter	(See Athlone)				
Strokestown (see Bumlin)	EL	1811-1971	1811-1919	1811-1985	RCBL
Tarmonbarry	EL		1846-1917		RCBL
Taughboy & Dysart	EL				Destroyed
Tessaragh	EL		1847-1930		RCBL
Tibohine	EL		1856-1955		RCBL
Toomna (Battlebridge)	EL				Destroyed

* Burgess (Rev. J.B.): Typescript copy, with indexes, of records of Kiltoom Church of Ireland parish, Co. Roscommon, containing Vestry minutes, 1788-1886, baptisms, 1797-1943, marriages, 1802-1910, burials, 1801-1943. Jan. 1944. NLI n.5205 p.5309

Methodist Records: Before 1820 Methodists were included in the Church of Ireland parish registers. They did not maintain their own graveyards or burial records. Information on the form of Methodist records is available in the chapter by M. Kelly & Roddie's "Methodist Records in Ireland," in *Irish Church Records*, Flyleaf Press, Dublin, 2001 (www.flyleaf.ie). See also www.irishmethodist.org/. The RHGC have indexed Methodist records from the early 1840s.

Presbyterian Records: Most surviving Presbyterian registers begin only in the nineteenth century and burial registers were not kept at all, until the present century.[9] In 1861, there were only 1,826 Presbyterians in Roscommon. Between 1868 and 1961 only 74 christenings were conducted for 30 families. These are listed in the *Roscommon Historical and Archaeological Society Journal*, Vol. 8, 2000, pp 101-102. The RHGC has indexed Presbyterian records, which start between 1857 and 1861. Further information can also be obtained on the website www.presbyterianireland.org/.

Society of Friends, or Quaker, Records: Quakers kept detailed records, but there was little Quaker activity in Roscommon. In 1717 and 1739 Quaker congregations settled at Ballymurry.[10] Further information is on the website www.quakers-in-ireland.org/.

Roman Catholic Records: Roman Catholic parish registers are almost all in the custody of the local parish church. The *Irish Catholic Directory* provides contact details of each parish. The website www. local.ie/general/genealogy/roman_catholic_registers is also useful. Researchers may write to the "Resident Priest" but remember they have limited time and a small donation is much appreciated. As the records are indexed by RHGC (see Table p.42) who also offer a search service. (see Chapter 18) some priests may refuse to use their time for a service which is available elsewhere.

The records are also on microfilm in the NLI and in LDS libraries. The quality of the microfilm records ranges from very poor to good. This is partly due to the quality of the original registers at the time of microfilming, and also because microfilming was not always of a high quality.

Another source is 'Marriages in the RC Diocese of Tuam 1821-29' which is an index of approx 4,000 marriages for Tuam diocese from

NLI P4222. These marriages are not included in the registers at parish level. This source has been published by Heritage Books (see below).

> McDermot Peter m Sarah Mullany
> 22 December 1823 in Kilvine
> Wits Con & Mary Mullany
>
> McDermott Andrew m Celia Prendergast
> 17 February 1822 in Kiltullagh
> Wits Michael McDermott & Mary Davis
>
> McDermott Cormack m Honor Rohan
> January 1827 (3) in Annadown
> Wits Rev Wm Mannion & Eleanor M---
>
> McDermott James m Bridget Kindrigan
> 14 November 1825 in Aughagowr
> Wits John & Patt Kindrigan
>
> McDermott James m Mary Brady
> 25 July 18224 in Kilcoleman
> Wits Matthew Prendergast & Peter Griffin
>
> McDermott Jno m Cathleen McDermt
> 20 February 1823 in Templetoher

'Marriages in the RC Diocese of Tuam 1821-29' (Heritage Books 1993)

Baptism registers record the name of the child, name and address of the father, maiden name of the mother, names of the sponsors, and the date. Marriage records show the name of the officiating priest, the date, names of the groom and bride and witnesses. They were recorded either in Latin or in English. Where Latin was used, it does not take too long to understand the key words such as "baptizatus" for baptized, "matrimonium" for married, and "sepultus" for buried.

The following table lists the RC parishes and the extent and location of their records. If parish of interest is not listed, it may have been consolidated into another parish. The column on the left indicates the Civil Parish in which each church is located.

o   Column 1:   Roman Catholic Parish, & Civil Parish in which it is located
o   Columns 2-4:   Dates of baptism, marriage and burial records.
o   Column 5.   Location of records, and ref. See abbreviations list. Familysearch is www.familysearch.org

Roman Catholic Church Records and Locations

Roman Catholic Parish, *Civil Parish*	Baptisms	Marriages	Burials	Location
Aghanagh. *CP: Aghanagh (partly in Co. Sligo)*	1803-1880	1800- 1880	1800-02; 1816; 1822-46; 1858-74	NLI & LDS 0989739; & 0989740 SHGC
Ardcarne & Tumna (Cootehall) *CP: Ardcarn*	1803-1899 1843-1880 1843-1900	1860-1899 1843- 1860; 1861- 1880 1843-1900		NLI & LDS 0989746 RHGC
Athleague & Fuerty *CP: Athleague*	1842-1900 1808-1900 1808-1828; 1834-1880	1863-1900 1808-1900 1808-1834; 1836-1878	1808-1837 1807-1837	EGFHS RHGC NLI
Ballinasloe (Creagh & Kilclooney): CP: Kilcloony	1820-1900 1820-1900 1820-1880	1853-1902 1820-1900 1820-1841	1825-1830 1820-1841	LDS 1279217 EGFHS NLI
Ballintubber & Ballymoe (Ballinakill & Kilcrone) *CPs: Ballintober & Drumatemple*	1831-1880 1831-1900	1831-1880 1831-1900		NLI RHGC

Boyle *CP: Boyle*	1793-1900 1793-1796; 1803-1806; 1811; 1814-80	1792-1900 1792-1797; 1803-1804; 1808-1880	1848-1864 1848- 1964	RHGC NLI & LDS 0989743
Castlemore &Kilcolman: *CPs: Castlemore &* *Kilcolman*	1851-1900 1851-1911 1851-1900 1851-1880	1830-1900 1830-1963 1830-1880		RHGC LDS 1279232 SHGC Items 1-9 NLI
Cloontuskert *CP: Cloontuskert*	1865-1880 1865-1900	1865-1879; 1865-1900		NLI & LDS 0989747 RHGC
Dysart & Tissara *CP: Dysart*	1850-1880 1850-1900	1862- 1880; 1862-1900	1862-1865	NLI & LDS 0989755 RHGC
Elphin & Creeve *CP: Elphin*	1807-1860; 1866-1880 1808-1900	1807-1880 1807-1900	1807-1838	NLI RHGC
Geevagh *CP: Kilmactranny*	1873-1899 1873-1880	1851-1899 1851-1880		SHGC NLI

Parish				
Kilbegnet & Glinsk *CP: Dunamon*	1836-1900	1836-1880 1836-1900	1836-1839 1836-1839	NLI RHGC
Kilbride *CP: Kilbride*	1835-1849 1868-1880 1835-1900	1838-1846 1838-1900		NLI & LDS 0989749 RHGC
Kilcorkey & Frenchpark (Belenagare). *CP: Kilcorkey*	1865-1880 1865-1900	1865-1900		NLI RHGC
Kilglass & Rooskey *CP: Kilglass*	1865- 1880 1865-1900	1865-1900 Pre-1850		NLI RHGC Williams
Kilkeevin or Kilkeevan *CP: Kilkeevan*	1804-1809 1816-1819 1826-1880 1804-1900	1804-09; 1816-19; 1838-80 1804-1900	1805-1809; 1816-1819; 1852-1855 1805-1855	NLI RHGC
Kilmore & Aughrim *CP: Aughrim*	1816-1880 1816-1900	1816-1880; 1816-1900		NLI RHGC

Parish				Sources
Kilnamanagh (Breedogue, Estersnow & Ballinameen). *CP: Kilnamanagh*	1859-1880 1859-1900	1860-1880 1860-1900		NLI & Familysearch LDS 0989738/ BIVRI, Online RHGC
Kilronan. (Keadue. Arigna & Ballyfarnon). *CP: Kilronan*	1824-1829; 1835-1876 1824-1900 1824-1829; 1835-1976	1823-1829 1835-1872 1823-1900	1835-1872 1835-1872	NLI RHGC LDS 1279224
Kiltomb or Kiltoom & Cam or Camma (Ballybay). *CP: Kiltoom*	1835-1845; 1848-1864 1835-1900	1835-1846; 1848-1880 1835-1900	1837-1845; 1857-1862; 1865 1837-1865	NLI & LDS 0989751 & Online Familysearch RHGC
Kiltrustan, Lissonuffy & Cloonfinlough (Strokestown) *CPs: Bumlin & Lissonuffy*	1830-1900 1830- 1880	1830-1900 1830-1880		RHGC NLI & LDS 0989745
Kiltulla or Kiltullagh *CP: Kiltullagh*	1839-1900 1839 -1880	1839-1900 1839- 1880		RHGC NLI & LDS 0926226

Parish / CP				Source
Killukin & Killumod (Boyle) *CP: Killukin (1)*	1811–1880 1811–1900	1825–1880 1825–1900	1820–1826	NLI & LDS 0989741 RHGC
Loughglynn & Lisacul (Tibohine). also part Frenchpark. *CP: Tibohine*	1817–1826; 1829–1840; 1849–1863; 1865–1880 1817–1900	1817–1836 1840–1849 1858; 1865– 1880; 1817–1900	1850–1854; 1868–1880 1850–1880 1849–1900	NLI & LDS 0989753 Familysearch; Part BIVRI/Online RHGC
Moore *CP: Moore*	1876–1938 1876–1900 1876–1880	1877–1880		LDS 1279214 RHGC NLI
Ogulla & Baslic (Kilmurry or Tulsk) *CP: Ogulla*	1865–1880 1865–1900	1869–1880 1865–1900		NLI RHGC
Oran (Cloverhill). *CP: Oran*	Not microfilmed 1864–1900	1864–1900		RHGC

Parish	Baptisms	Marriages	Burials	Source
Roscommon & Kilteevan *CP: Roscommon*	1837-1880 1820-1900	1820-1864 1820-1900	1821-1824	NLI & LDS 0989748 & Online Familysearch RHGC
Rooskey – see Kilglass				
St. John's (Killinvoy) *CP: Killinvoy*	1841-1880 1841-1900	1841-1880 1841-1900	1854-1880 1854-1881	NLI & LDS 0989752 RHGC
St. Peter's & Drum *CP: St. Peter's (Athlone)*	1789-1880 1789-1900	1789-1880 1789-1900	1789-1880 1789-1880	NLI & LDS 0989738/ Online Familysearch RHGC
Taughmaconnell. *CP: Taughmaconnell*	1842-1880 1842-1900 1842-1880	1863-1880 1842-1900 1863-1880		LDS 0926061 RHGC NLI
Tibohine *CP: Tibohine*	1833-1900 1833-1900	1833-1900 1833-1880		RHGC NLI

VALUATION OF TENEMENTS.
PARISH OF KILTOOM.

No. and Letter of Reference to Map.	Townlands and Occupiers.	Immediate Lessors.	Description of Tenement.	Area. A. B. P.	Rateable Land. £ s. d.	Rateable Buildings. £ s. d.	Total Annual Valuation of Rateable Property. £ s. d.
	KNOCKNANOOL— *continued.*						
1 — d	John Doolan,	Timothy Lynch,	House and garden,	0 1 20	0 5 0	0 5 0	0 10 0
— e	William Bryan,	Same,	House,	0 2 32	0 10 0	0 5 0	0 15 0
11 — a	Mary Gaffey,	Reps. Daniel Farrell,	House, offices, and land,	23 1 32	7 0 0	1 0 0	8 5 0
12 — b	John Cunningham,	Maurice Gaffey,	House and garden,	0 3 7	0 10 0	0 5 0	0 15 0
	Reps. Daniel Farrell,	In fee,	Bog,	08 2 9	0 10 0	—	0 10 0
			Total,	370 1 35	93 0 0	20 17 0	113 17 0
	LISBAUN. (Ord. S. 48.)						
1 — a	Hugh Martin,	Sir Frederick Trench,	Land,	9 0 0	4 15 0	—	4 15 0
2	Thomas Feluily,	Same,	House and land,	8 1 20	4 5 0	0 10 0	4 15 0
3	John Lenihan,	Same,	House and land,	25 2 11	15 10 0	1 0 0	16 10 0
4 — A } — B	James Killeen,	Same,	Land,	8 0 20 / 38 0 35	4 5 0 / 15 0 0	—	} 10 5
5 — a	Patrick Healy,	James Killeen,	House,	18 2 33	10 15 0	0 15 0	0 15 0
6 — a	Patrick Murray,	Sir Frederick Trench,	House, offices, and land,	3 2 10	1 15 0	1 0 0	11 15 0
7 — a	Michael Kelly,	Same,	House and land,	17 0 25	8 0 0	0 5 0	2 0 0
8 — a	Patrick Harney,	Same,	House, offices, and land,	17 1 32	0 0 0	0 15 0	8 15 0
9 — a	Timothy Connolly,	Same,	House, office, and land,	0 3 10	0 10 0	0 10 0	0 15 0
— a	Patrick Connolly,	Same,	Land, House, offices, & land, }	13 1 5	5 0 0 } 4 10 0	1 0 0	} 6 0 0 / 5 10 0
{ a { b	Thomas Kelly, sen.,						

Page from Griffith Valuation for the Civil Parish of Kiltoom

Chapter 7   Land Records

Tracing ancestors is all about finding records of their existence. This chapter discusses how to search and use land records such as Griffith's Valuation, the "Cancelled Land Books" of the Valuation Office, Tithe Applotment Books and the Registry of Deeds.

Griffith's Valuation (1847-64): The Primary Valuation of Ireland, more commonly known as Griffith's Valuation provides the name of the occupier (head of household only) of land and buildings in every townland or street in the country. It also lists the names of those from whom the land is leased (the lessor), and the amount and taxable valuation of the land held (see p.48). Unlike the Tithe Applotment Books (see p.50), it also covers property in cities and towns. It was carried out between 1855 and 1858, to determine liability to pay a tax called a 'Poor Rate'.

Griffith's Valuation is available on microfiche in NLI and NAI. An index (see 'Index of Surnames' on p.51) and guide available in the NLI. It is also available by subscription on www.irishorigins.com. Researchers can also utilise CD-ROMs such as Grenham's Irish Surnames, Eneclann Ltd. 2003, and Family Tree Maker's Index to Griffith's Valuation of Ireland, 1848-1864, CD #188, Broderbund, 1998.

Field Books, House Books and Tenure Books: The NAI also holds the manuscript records of Griffith's survey, including the notebooks used by the surveyors. These record details of the properties and lands surveyed. The **Field Books** record the characteristics and productivity of the soil. The **House Books** provide details about the dwelling and building structures on each land holding. The **Tenure Books** provide information about whether the land was leased, and if so, the duration and nature.

Later Valuation Office Records: Records of changes of land ownership after the Primary Valuation are also available in the Valuation Office (see Chap. 18). The "Cancelled Land Books" and "Current Land Books" provide details of all changes in holdings and occupants up to the present time. The Valuation Office also holds the Ordnance Survey maps annotated /coloured to accompany the Valuation.

Extract from the Tithe Applotment Books for Brideswell Town

Tithe Applotment Books (1823-38): The Tithe Applotment Survey was compiled between 1823 and 1838 to determine the amount which occupiers of agricultural holdings should pay in tithes to the Church of Ireland. There is a manuscript book for every parish and townland, showing the names of occupiers (the head of households), the amount of land held, and the sums to be paid (see p.50). The originals of the Tithe Applotment Books are held at the NAI, and copies are in the NLI and in Roscommon County Library. The NLI has also compiled an index of surnames (see below).

Some caveats in using the Tithe Applotment Books include the fact that there can be more than one listing for the one person. A second and more difficult problem is that the Tithe lists did not include all households. Some land was exempt from tithes and sometimes the tithes were paid by one named person on behalf of others. This was often the case where families had subdivided a farm. Some names are thus lost.

The Index of Surnames: The NLI has compiled a joint index of surnames listed in either the Griffith Valuation and Tithe Applotment Surveys. It is available in the NLI Catalogue Room and at the NAI and (for Roscommon only) at Roscommon County Library. It also includes a list of parishes for which no Tithe Books were received. This index is helpful where the exact place of residence of an ancestor within the county is uncertain. It will identify where those with a particular surname lived and the spelling variations for the name in Roscommon and neighbouring counties. For example the name Hamrock (and variants) are listed as follows:

Mayo			**Barony**
Amroge	G 2		Clanmorris
Annage	G		Clanmorris
Hamrock	G 2	T	Costello
Hamrogue	G 7	T	Kilmaine
Roscommon			**Barony**
Hamrock	G 7	T	Athlone

In Roscommon, this indicates that the name Hamrock is listed seven times (G7) in Griffith's in the Barony of Athlone, and that it is also listed (T) in this Barony in the Tithe Applotment Survey. The researcher can then use further layers of the index to establish the exact location of each holding, and also the extent and leasehold nature of the land held.

Registry of Deeds: A deed is a legal agreement between two parties. Legally this agreement can be on any matter, but in practice the vast majority deal with land transfer. From 1708, Deeds were required to be registered in order to be legal, and hence a Registry of Deeds was created in Dublin (see Chapter 18) and is still in operation. Deeds are mainly, but not exclusively, relevant to the landed families and thus ignore a very large part of the Roscommon population. They are valuable because the parties to deeds are often described by their relationship (e.g. Michael Burke, son of Roderick Burke ..). Addresses and occupations are also often provided. Many deal with transfers of property or other agreements within extended families and therefore describe interrelationships. They may also list names of owners of adjoining properties (commonly used in defining land boundaries), existing tenants within properties, and witnesses.

Research in the Registry of Deeds can be time consuming, but it is a fascinating repository. There are two sets of indexes to Deeds:

o   **Grantors Indexes**: Index to persons selling or leasing land. These are in handwritten volumes identified by initial letter of surname and date, e.g., C 1708-1738. The Index lists: Surname and forename of grantor; surname (only) of the grantee; and reference information to locate the original deed.
o   **Land Index**: Index to townland, parish etc in which the land is located. This is often useful where the name of the grantor may be unknown.

Pre-1708 Deeds: A small collection of pre 1708 deeds for County Roscommon is held at the NAI. These were made before the creation of the Registry of Deeds. A card index is available, arranged by barony. Further collections of Roscommon Deeds are also noted at the end of Chapter 8.

Encumbered Estates: In 1849 a Court was established to sell the estates of insolvent or 'encumbered' owners. Pre-sale promotional information was published on each auctioned estate, often including names of current tenants. Various indexes exist in the NLI and NAI.

The Land Commission: The Irish Land Commission was created in 1881 to determine fair rents. Later it developed into a tenant-purchasing commission and assisted in the transfer of 13.5 million acres from landlord to tenant. The commission was reconstituted by the Land Law (Commission) Act, 1923. In 1983 it ceased acquiring land, and was dissolved in 1999. Most of the remaining assets and records were transferred to the Minister for Agriculture and Food, and many historical records are now held by the NAI.

Documents of title make up a significant portion of the Land Commission's material. These include descriptions of the land being transferred and an abstract of the seller's title to the land, including deeds, mortgages, and wills.[11] The NLI holds two Land Commission card indexes: (1) by estate and (2) by vendor. The NLI also holds an index to wills held by the Land Commission. The Land Commission holds a large collection of land records, but permission must be sought to obtain access (see Chapter 18). It is recommended that researcher either write to or telephone the NAI, contact details provided in Chapter 18, before conducting a visit to review Land Commission records.

The Land Registry: The Land Registry was established in 1892 to provide a system of compulsory registration of title of land. It records the current owner of all land in Roscommon or elsewhere. All title and map records for Roscommon are held by the Land Registry, Nassau Building, Setanta Centre, Dublin 2. The website and email contact details of the Land Registry are www.landregistry.ie/ and info@landregistry.ie, repectively.

Estate Owner	House name and Location	Acres
H. King Harmon	Rockingham, near Boyle	29,242
H.S. Pakenham Mahon	Strokestown Park House,	26,980
Lord De Freyne	Frenchpark,	25,436
Sandford, Thomas J.	Willsgrove, Mount Sandford	24,410
Edward Tenison		16,915
Colonel French		12,270
Lord Crofton	Mote Park House, Lisdorne	10,509
O'Conor Don	Clonalis, Castlereagh	10,467
John Chidley Coote	Cootehall	10,318
William Lloyd	Crohan	7,394
Guy Lloyd	Lissadurn, Elphin area	7,302
Arthur O'Conor		6,927
Patrick Balfe	Glanballythomas	6,024
William T. Potts	Newcourt, Athlone	5,813
William C. Kyle		5,589
John T. Dillon		5,588
Viscount Dillon	Loughglinn	5,430
Thomas William Goff	Oakport House	5,429
John Murphy	Mullen and Reheely	5,362
H. Taffe Ferrall		5,140
Total		**232,545**

The twenty largest estates in Roscommon in 1876 [12]

Chapter 8   Estate Records

In the eighteenth and nineteenth centuries the vast majority of the population lived as small tenant-farmers on large estates owned for the most part by English or Anglo-Irish landlords. An indication of the landlords' names, estate locations and area sizes of the twenty largest Roscommon estates for the year 1876 is provided in the table opposite.

Over 232,000 acres or 37% of land was owned by 20 families.[13] Note also that less than 20% of these landlords had native Irish surnames, showing that most economic and political power rested with Anglo-Irish landed families.

The administration of these estates inevitably produced large quantities of records – maps, tenants' lists, rentals, account books, lease books, etc.[14] These records are potentially a valuable source for eighteenth century research. Estate records take more effort to locate, but if found the information they contain can be very worthwhile. They are not only a primary source of information on landowner families, but may be the only record of the existence of tenant farmers in this period.

Old estates have now been broken up and family papers dispersed to governmental or private archives, solicitors' offices, or to the dump. The Irish Manuscripts Commission (IMC) foresaw the possible loss of valuable papers and conducted various surveys of private collections.[15] Since the publication of Pomfret's *The Struggle for land in Ireland, 1800-1923* in 1930, estate records have started to become more widely available. These records have enlightened historians as to what actually occurred on estates in terms of rent increases, estate improvements, and evictions.[16]

To conduct research on estate papers you must (1) identify the landlord of the property occupied by an ancestor and (b) establish whether estate papers exist and, if so, where.

Identifying the Landlord: This may be done by consulting the 'Immediate Lessors' column in *Griffith's Valuation* (see Chapter 7). Note, however, that the 'Immediate Lessor' may have been a tenant or agent who was in turn letting the land. It is important to review the 'Immediate Lessor' column carefully to see if he or she is in turn a tenant of another 'Immediate Lessor'. When the landlord's name is identified, researchers can consult several possible sources. One is the *Return of Owners of Land of One Acre and Upwards, in the Several Counties, Counties of Cities, and Counties of Towns in Ireland,* Dublin, 1876. A second resource is *The Landowners of Ireland* by O.H. Hussey de Burgh (1878) which lists major landowners, and size and location of their holdings.

Local histories of an area will often indicate major local landowners. For the nineteenth century, a variety of gazetteers and directories are available which offer some information on landowners in the area (see Chapter. 11).

Locating the Estate Records: When the landlord has been identified, there are several works which can assist in finding the estate records. One of the first indexes to consult should be Richard Hayes's *Manuscript Sources for the Study of Irish Civilisation* and its supplements (see Chapter 14) If no records can be traced at a public repository, it is worth investigating whether an estate's solicitors are still in business. They may hold family papers or know their whereabouts or be may be able to put the researcher in contact with descendants of the landed family who may still retain at least some of the estate records. Descendants may also be traced by using the most recent editions of works such as *Burke's Landed Gentry of Ireland* or *Debrett's Peerage and Baronetage.* Local libraries, heritage centres and archives may also be worth consulting for estate papers. For example, Clonalis House, located in County Roscommon, contains one of the greatest collections of Irish manuscripts still in private hands.[17] Clonalis House is the ancestral home of the O'Conors, Kings of Connacht, and at various times, High Kings of Ireland. The 'New' Clonalis House now serves the dual purpose of being a family home and a major repository of heritage and history, containing correspondence, heirlooms, *objet d'art* and portraits of the O'Conors over the past 600 years.

Information and records of estates which transferred to tenants with the assistance of the Land Commission are located in the NAI. Mr.

Edward Keane was commissioned by the NLI in the 1970s to conduct a survey of these estates. An index is in the NLI even though the records themselves are held in the Land Commission office, within the NAI. Documents of title make up a significant part of this collection. These consist of a description of the lands being sold and an abstract of the vendor's title to the land, including deeds, wills, mortgages etc.

The following is a list of some County Roscommon landowner families with description of some of their estate papers and where they are located.

Balfe (see also Berington): Worcester: Record Office: Mss.705: 24/1795-1857: Berington papers, relating mainly to estates in Cos. Roscommon ... of the Balfe family, mostly of the period 1840-90, but containing some earlier papers. NLI n.2452 p.1532.

Worcester: Record Office: Mss.705: 24/1805-6: Rentals & other papers relating to lands in Glanballythomas, Co. Roscommon, 1854-65. Letters re Glans & Runnimede estates, with incidental papers, 1859-61. NLI n.2452-3 p.1532-3.

NAI M. 2593: Valuation survey of the Balfe estate in Cos. Roscommon & Sligo, 1858.

Berington: Worcester: Record Office: Mss. 705: 24/1813-14, 1817: Rentals of estates of .... Rathconnelly, Co. Roscommon. 1864-5. n.2452 p.1532.

Bond: Trinity College Library Dublin: Mss. 4255-56 (Q.9.12-13): Account of origins, lease book, of the ? Bond estate in Co. .... Roscommon, Westmeath, c. 1778-1855

Frances Boswell: NLI pos. (microfilm) 4937, Rent ledger, c.1760-86, major tenants only, covering townlands in the civil parish of Kilronan.

John Browne of Moyne: NLI 16 I. 14(6) MS map: Cloonagloshy, Co. Roscommon. Octavo sheet, 1801.

NLI 16 I. 14(7) Ms map: Cloonagloshy (Co. Roscommon?), copied from a map made by John Evans, for the use of John Browne of Moyne, by John Hanly. Nov., 1798.

NLI 16 I. 14 (8) A map of Carroanaskagh, the estate of John Browne of Moyne, in the parish of Cloonfinlogh, Co. Roscommon with names of tenants, August, 1811.

NLI 16 I. 14 (9) A map of Moyne, the estate of John Browne of Moyne, in the parish of Cloonfinlogh, barony & co. of Roscommon with names of tenants, August, 1811. Also an accurate map of lands of Moher ..., by H. Hanly. Quarto sheet, Aug., 1811.

Bruen: NLI Ms. 10,079: Documents in the case of Richard St. George v. Bruen concerning lands in counties Roscommon & Leitrim, late 18th c.

Bucknall:NLI D. 27,276: Mortgage by Robert Hart to Charles Bucknall relating to lands at Baslick, barony of Ballintober, Co. Roscommon, 8 Jul. 1775.

Caulfield: Ms map: Map of the estate of Capt. Caulfield French in the townlands of Castleteheen & Kiltulogue, Co. Roscommon. Folio sheet, 1906. NLI 15 A. 20 (12).

NLI 21 F. 125: 15 coloured maps of the estate of Col. W. Caulfield, ... Roscommon & Westmeath with names of tenants, 1811-1837.

NLI Ms. 3154: Accounts of .. Col. Caulfield's estate in Carnaglass (Co. Roscommon?), 1802-1822.

NLI Ms map: Map of the estate of Capt. Caulfield French in townlands of Castleteheen & Kiltultogue, Co. Roscommon. Folio sheet, 1906. 15 A. 20 (13).

Cleaver: James Hardiman Library, NUI Galway, Ms. LE2, Cleaver Estates, 1834-1840; Account Book of John Carson, agent of Rev. William Cleaver, administration of the estate which covers the townlands of Cam, Attroy, Kilcorky, Ikearon, & Lissyallen, all in County Roscommon, 135 pages

Clonbrock/ Dillon: NLI Ms. 19, 501, Tenants' ledgers, 1801-1806, indexed, covering townlands in the civil parish of Taughmaconnell of Luke Dillon, 2nd Baron Clonbrock

NLI Ms. 19585-19608, 1827-1840, Rentals & accounts of the estates of Robert Dillon, 3rd Baron Clonbrock, Counties Galway & Roscommon. There are 24 volumes in total.

Connolly (Castletown): Irish Architectural Archive; Collection: Castletown Papers; references 97/84/Box 4, 1703-1780; Deeds referring to lands in Cos. .... Roscommon

Irish Architectural Archive; Collection: Castletown Papers; references 97/84/Box 78, 1694-1840; Leases, letters & legal documents referring to lands in Cos. .… Roscommon.

Coote: NAI M. 3045: Survey of estates in Cos. … Roscommon & Leitrim of Sir C.H. Coote, 1819.

Edward Crofton: NLI M. 19672, Rent roll, May 1778, major tenants only… in the civil parishes of Baslick, Estersnow, Kilbryan, Kilgefin, Killinvoy, Killumod, Kilmeane, Kiltrustan, Ogulla

Humphrey Crofton. NLI Ms. 4531, Rental, March 1833, tenants' names alphabetically, covering townlands in the civil parish of Tumna.

Crofton: Mote Park, Ballymurray – collection of records held at National Library

James Hardiman Library, NUI Galway, Ms. LE1, Crofton Estates, 1833-1840; Account Book of John Carson, agent for Lord Crofton, relating to estates inc. the townlands of Ballymurry, Ballinree, Corbally, Culeenbag, Carnamadda, Moneymore, etc., all in Co. Roscommon, 155 pages.

NLI Ms. 19,672: Clonbrock Papers: Maps of estate of Edward Crofton, Esq., in Co. Roscommon, by Charles Frizell, No. 1777. 35 coloured maps, mainly 11" X 9", with accompanying lists of tenants' holdings & observations thereon, also rent roll for the estates, May, 1778.

NLI Mss. 8826-8827, Rentals & legal documents, 18th & early 19th century, of the estates of Lord Crofton, Counties Sligo & Roscommon

NAI, M. 937 x 940x, 941x; Rentals c. 1850 & maps, 1833-40, of the Crofton estate in Co. Roscommon & Sligo

Ms maps: Maps of the estate of Lord Crofton situated in the baronies of Athlone & Ballintubber, South Co. Roscommon, with ms. & printed documents in relation to Landed Property Improvement .… Folio volume, 3 printed & 4 ms. maps, coloured, 1853-73. NLI 21 F. 1

NLI Ms maps: Maps of the estate of Lord Crofton in Co. Roscommon. By various surveyors. 16 maps, coloured in outline & in full, 1724-c. 1850. 21 F 23 (1-16).

NLI Ms. 3499: Farm account book, apparently of a Crofton family estate in Co. Roscommon, 1871-1875.

NLI Mss. 4054-4055: Two account books of estate of Lord Crofton of Mote, 1841-1853 & 1866-1867.

NAI. M. 3740 (1-8): Papers relating to dealings of Land Commission with estates in Co. Roscommon of Lord Crofton, 1907-9.

NLI M. 3918: Rental of Lord Crofton's estates in Co. Roscommon & statement of expenditure on his behalf by Joseph A. Homses, 1878.

NLI Mss. 4074-4079: Six rentals & accounts of Lord Crofton's Co. Roscommon estates compiled by his agent, Joseph A. Homses, 1862-1868.

NLI Mss. 4081-4100: Twenty rentals & accounts of Lord Crofton's Co. Roscommon estates provided by Joseph A. Homses & W.B. Talbot-Crosbie, agents, 1868-1892.

NLI Mss. 4101-4102: Rentals of Lord Crofton's Roscommon estate & accounts furnished by W.D. Talbot Crosbie …., 1892-1893 & 1894-1895.

NLI Mss. 3043-3046: Four farm account books of estate of Lord Crofton of Mote, Co. Roscommon, 1866-1875.

NLI Ms. 4056-4064: Nine farm stock account books of Lord Crofton of Mote park, Co. Roscommon, 1837-1893.

NLI Mss. 5632-5633: Rentals of the estate of Lord Crofton in County Roscommon for the years 1852 & 1855, together with expenditure accounts for the years, 1852-53 & 1855-56.

NLI Ms. 5904: Survey of Lord Crofton estate in Roscommon, 1782 & rental, 1844-1845.

NLI Ms. 19,672: Clonbrock Papers: Maps of estate of Edward Crofton, Esq., in Co. of Roscommon, by Charles Frisell, Nov. 1777. 35 coloured maps, mainly 11" X 9", with accompanying lists of tenants' holdings & observations thereon, also rent roll, May 1778.

De Freyne or **French** (See also Caulfield): Frenchpark records held at NLI

NLI Ms maps: Maps of Lord De Freyne's estate, 22 townlands in baronies of Frenchpark, Castlereagh & Ballymoe, Co. Roscommon. 1906. 15 A. 20(3-7).

Dalton: (see Hanly)

Dillon (see also Hanly) : NLI Ms map: Map of the Dillon estate in townlands of Carrigan Beg & Carrigan More, Co. Roscommon & ... Co. Westmeath. Two folio sheets, 1907. 15 A. 20 (8-9).

Oxford: Co. Record Office: Mss. Dil. XXII. a. 1-5: Dillon Papers. List of articles sent from Loughglin to Dublin, Oct. 1795. Plans for proposed alterations to Loughglin House ...., 19th c. Ordnance survey maps of Dillon estates, Loughglin (Co. Roscommon).... 19th c. NLI n. 5208 p. 5312.

COLONEL HENRY DILLON'S INFANTRY.   583

COLONEL HENRY DILLON.

THIS name is of record in Ireland from the time of the Invasion, immediately after which Sir Henry Dillon, styled of Drumrany, had from King John large grants over that portion of Western Meath and Annaly, which was thence called the Dillon's Country. His descendants were Barons of Kilkenny West, and subsequently ennobled as Earls of Roscommon, Viscounts Dillon and Mayo, and Barons of Clonbrock. In the sixteenth century the name of Dillon is conspicuous on the Roll of the Judicial Officers of Ireland. In 1532, Sir Bartholomew Dillon was appointed Chief Justice of the King's Bench. In 1554, Robert Dillon, of Newtown near Trim was named a Justice of the Queen's Bench, and advanced in 1559 to the Chief Justiceship of the Common Pleas. In 1560, Richard Dillon of Proutestown, County of Meath, became a Justice of the Queen's Bench. In 1570, Sir Lucas Dillon was Chief Baron of the Exchequer. In 1581, Robert Dillon, of Riverston, County of Westmeath, was second Justice of the Common Pleas. In 1590, Gerald Dillon was a Justice of the Queen's Bench. In two years after, Thomas Dillon, theretofore Chief Justice of Connaught, was appointed a Justice of the Common Pleas ; and in 1638, Robert Lord Dillon was one of the Keepers of the Great Seal.

A page from 'King James's Irish Army List 1689
by John D'Alton (Dublin 1855)

Oxford: Co. Record Office: Ms. Dil. XXII, C. 2: Dillon Papers: Book containing list of officers & men in the Loughglin cavalry, embodied 1796. NLI n. 5208 p. 5312.

Oxford: Co. Record Office: Ms. Dil. XXII, b. 14: Dillon Papers: Letters to Viscount Dillon on estate matters from his agent, Charles Strickland, 1854-5 & from Alfred Markby, June, 1887 & Dec., 1890. NLI n. 5208 p. 5312.

Oxford: Co. Record Office: Mss. Dil. XXII b. 7-9: Dillon Papers: Book of leases of Irish estates of Viscount Dillon, 1805. Statement & report of Mr. Strickland, agent in Ireland, for Visct. Dillon, 1832. Account of remittances by Mr. Strickland, agent to Visct. Dillon, out of Irish rents, 1835-7. NLI n.5208 p.5312.

Dolling: NAI 329a: Map … of estate of Caledon Dolling in Lisalway, Co. Roscommon, 1890.

Domvile: Map showing proposed road at Moyvannan (Co. Roscommon), the property of Sir Charles W.C. Domvile. By J.F. Kempster. Folio sheet, partly coloured, 1860. NLI 21 F. 103 (7).

Duckworth: NAI, M. 1200: Rental of the Duckworth Estate in Co. Roscommon, 1864

Sir Thomas Dundas: NLI Ms. 10152 & NLI Mss.2787, 2788, Rentals, 1792 & 1804, major tenants only. in the civil parishes of Boyle, Estersnow, Kilnamanagh, & Tumna.

NLI Special List 223 Estate Papers Roscommon & Sligo, Dundas Family.

NLI Ms. 2786: Rental of the estate of Sir Thomas Dundas in cos Roscommon & Sligo & observations on the state of the land by Walter Dawson. With index of names, 1783.

NLI Ms. 2787-2788: Rentals of the estate of Sir Thomas Dundas in cos of Roscommon & Sligo, 1792 & 1804.

Erwin: NAI Ms. 545: Survey of plots held by widow Erwin in Castlerea, by A. Higgins, 1769.

Walker Evans NLI Ms 10152, Leases, c.1790, rentals & leases of tenants in townlands in civil parish of Creeve.

Fitzgibbon: NLI Ms map: Map of the farm of John Fitzgibbon in Townlands of Listhomasroe & Carrowkeel, Co. Roscommon. Folio sheet, 1907. 15 A. 20(10).

Fitzmaurice Papers (see also Hodson): NLI. Ms. 23,256, 1797-1824, Rent Ledger & Account Book of Lt. Edward Hodson, Royal City Dublin Militia, with reference to land in Counties Galway & Roscommon

French (see also De Freyne & Caulfield) NAI D. 17,222-6: Papers re estates in Cos. Roscommon ….of the French family, with references to families of Ross & Gethin, 1810-62.

NLI Ms maps: Maps of lands in baronies of Frenchpark, Moycarn & Roscommon, Co. Roscommon. 39 maps, 1716-1838. 21 F. 45 (79-116)

NAI M. 3035: Receiver's accounts for the estate of R.H. French in Shragh & Derrylahan, Castlereagh barony, Roscommon, 1820-1, 1841.

Glancy/Glancey: NLI Ms map: Map showing the Mary Glancy estate in the townland of Bohagh, Co. Roscommon, 1906. 15 A. 20 (2).

NLI Ms map: Map showing Col. Glancey's estate in townland of Willsgrove, Co. Roscommon. One sheet, 1907. 15 A. 20(1).

Gordon: NLI Ms map: Map of the farm of James Gordon in the townland of Lisgarve, Co.Roscommon. Folio sheet, 1906. 15 A. 20 (13).

Greville: NAI. M. 3050: Papers re estates of the Greville family in Co. Cavan, 19th c. & survey of the estates of Col. Fulke Southwell Greville in Co. Roscommon.

Gunning: NLI Ms.10152, Rental, 1792, major tenants only, rentals covering townlands in the civil parishes of Athleague, Fuerty, Kilcooley.

Handcock   (see King-Harman)

Hanly: NLI Ms. 24,597 (1) – (2). Deeds re land transactions in Roscommon including those by Dalton, Dillon, but mainly Hanly families ca. 1650-1700.

Hanly Papers: Wages books of Patrick Hanly of Carrowcrin, Co. Roscommon, with notes on farming operations, 1838-41. N.4918 p.4950.

Hanly papers: Volume containing labourers' wages, 1845-50 & farm accounts, 1841-3 of Patrick Hanly of Carrowcrin, Co. Roscommon. N.4918 p.4950.

Hatley Manor: See St George

Harris: NAI M. 320: Map … of estate of T. Harris in Callow, Killnamannagh parish, Co. Roscommon, 1747.

Hodson: See Fitzmaurice

Holmes: NAI M. 3694: Map & rental of estate of Lily Holmes in Cloonlaughnan, Athlone Barony, Co. Roscommon, n.d.

NAI D. 20,902: M. 3694 (1-51): Papers dealing with estate in Cloonlaughman, Athlone Barony, Co. Roscommon of Lily Holmes, 19th c.

Hughes: PRONI D. 2946 add.: Maps of Hughes' estate, Co. Roscommon etc, 19th c.

Hyde: Ms. 18,261: Agreements of occupiers of Banada Morris & Keelbanada, Co. Roscommon, reserving shooting rights to Douglas Hyde; 3 items covering period 1893-1910.

Irwin: See Erwin and Mahon

Johnson (née Hughes): PRONI D/2269; C. 1805-1959; 300 documents inc. e.g., rentals & estate accounts of Lady Jane Johnson's (née Hughes) Roscommon estates, 1850s-1895; correspondence re estate of Lady Jane Johnson, Roscommon, 1845-1848; testamentary papers & papers re the personal estate of Margaret Hughes, Cloughfern, County Antrim, c. 1805-1959

Keogh: NAI M. 3010: Map of the Keogh estate in Co. Roscommon, 1797.

Keon: NAI Hoey & Denning, parcel 30: Papers re property in Co. Roscommon of W.I. Keon, C. 1897.

King (inc. King Harman & Kingston): NLI Ms. 3524: Accounts book of Rev. H. King of Ballylin, including executors' accounts & rent accounts concerning family estates in counties Leitrim, Roscommon & Offaly, 1825-1827.

NLI Ms. 4170, Rent rolls & accounts, 1801-1818, major tenants only, covering townlands in the civil parishes of Creeve, Elphin, Kilmore.

NLI Ms. 4120, Rent rolls & accounts, 1801-1818, major tenants only, in cos Roscommon, Leitrim & Offaly.

NLI 16 I 14(4) Ms map: Map of Curry in parish of Commough, Barony of Athlone, Co. Roscommon, the estate of John King. Surveyed by P. Mulvihill Oct. 1768.

NLI Ms. 3125: Rent & miscellaneous accounts book of the estate of John King (died 1778) in Counties Roscommon, Leitrim & Longford, 1757-1786.

Ms map: A collection of 15 maps of the estate of Sir Gilbert King in Leitrim, Roscommon & Sligo, by various surveyors. (8 ms maps, coloured & 7 Ordnance Survey maps), 1767-1862. NLI 16 F. 9.

Sligo Co. Library, King Estate, S./R., 1671-1827, Rentals of King-Kingston estates, 1671, 1697, & 1765; Rental & sale particulars of Lord Kingston's estate in baronies of Corron, Tirerrill, Tireragh, etc., 1826; Quit rents paid by Lord Lorton on his Sligo/Roscommon estates, 1827 (see also Lorton).

NLI Ms maps: A collection of 44 maps of estate of earl of Kingston in cos of Roscommon & Sligo. Taken from a map by Garret Hogan in 1724 …. Interleaved with table of reference. Folio sheets coloured in outline on vellum paper, 1765-70. 21 F. 13.

NLI 14 A 1-2, 182 maps of estates of Rt. Hon. King Harman NLI Mss. 14,103-9: 7 account books … detailing business of estates of … Rev. William Handcock, cos. Roscommon & Westmeath; 1845-late 19th c.

NLI 14 A 1-2, 182 coloured maps of the estates of the Rt. Hon. Harman King Harman in the County Roscommon. Two large folio volumes some with names of tenants.

NLI Ms. 3077, Rentals, 1845-66, townlands in civil parishes of Cloonfinlough, Rahara.

Knox: NLI Ms. Rental of Roscommon estate of Francis Blake Knox & Edward Ernest Knox, 1849-1886.

Lane / Fox: Leeds Public Libraries: Archives Dept.: L.F. C XIV. 1-2. Rental estates of James Fox in .. Co. Roscommon (Tulsk), 1819. Correspondence concerning the estate & list of tenants of the Dromahair estate of George Lane Fox, 1845. NLI n.4393 p.4064.

Lewis: NAI M.5637: Chancery orders March 26, 1842 & Oct. 8, 1845 for payment of rents of the estates of Arthur Gamble Lewis in Counties Roscommon & Leitrim.

Lillie: NLI 16 I 13 (1); Map of Drimdoe & Tintagh, in the barony of Boyle, Co. Roscommon, showing the property of Sir John Scott Lillie, Folio sheet, 1728.

Lloyd: NLI Ms. 19,022: Volume with survey & 14 maps of several townlands in part of the estate of Owen in the Lissadurn, Elphin area of Co. Roscommon; in colour & with names of occupiers, by Samuel Jones, 1821.

Lion: Ms map: Survey of Abby Carthron, Co. Roscommon, in the possession of Edmd; Lion of Elphin…and several others. By Fiagh Kelly, One paper sheet, …. June, 1717. NLI 16 I. 14(2).

Name of Owner.	Address of Owner.	Extent.			Valuation.	
		A.	R.	P.	£	s.
Broderick, Charles, .	Tarmon, Castlerea, .	514	1	25	99	10
Brooke, Thomas, now John Gore Young.	Ranelagh-road, Dublin,	139	1	30	49	15
Browne, Arthur, .	Mount Browne, Strokestown.	455	2	20	233	0
Browne, Ellen C.,	Clontarf, . . .	338	0	25	196	10
Browne, Very Rev. Dean.	Bennett's Bridge, Kilkenny.	360	0	0	245	15
Burke, E. H., .	Drum Park, Athlone, .	667	2	10	388	10
Burke, Gerald, .	Ballyhaunis, . .	73	2	20	40	10
Burke, J. M., . .	Ballinderry, . .	135	2	0	62	10
Burke, John, . .	Hollywell, Ballyhaunis,	29	0	10	9	5
Burke, John, . .	Carrowroe Park, Roscommon.	2,941	3	10	1,656	15
Burke, Sir Thomas, .	Marble Hill, Loughrea,	2,230	3	30	775	0
Burn, John, . .	Cartron, Athlone, .	150	3	10	69	0
Burns, Mrs. K. P., .	Aughnasurn, Boyle, .	338	3	20	113	10
Burton, Mrs. H., .	Kildurney, . .	104	1	20	59	15
Butler, Humphrey, Reps. of.	Shedfield Lodge, Farham, England.	628	2	0	263	15
Butson, Rev. C. H. G.,	Eyrecourt, . .	348	1	14	114	10
Byrne, Francis, .	Drumsua, . . .	290	3	30	260	2
Byrne, Mrs. G., . .	Drumana, . . .	379	1	33	321	18

Typical detail found in 'Land Owners in Ireland 1876' (Dublin 1876)

Longfield: NLI Ms maps: Maps of estate of R.O. Longfield in baronies of Athlone North & Frenchpark, Co. Roscommon. Two folio sheets, (1906). 15 A. 20(14-15).

Longworth: Ms maps: … maps containing, estates of George Longworth in Roscommon …. Surveyed & drawn by P. Blake, 1821. With map by J. Shadwell dated 1734 & a map enlarged from OS by W.H. Luscombe, 1850, Oblong quarto volume of 28 maps, 1734-1850. 14 A. 25.

Lord Lorton: NLI Ms. 3104-3105, Two lease books, 1740-1901, inc. many leases to small tenants in cos. Roscommon & Sligo, with lives mentioned, covering …. civil parishes of Ardcarn, Aughrim, Boyle, Creeve, Elphin, Estersnow, Kilbryan, Kilnamanagh.

Lucy: London: British Museum: Add. Charter, 7052: Mortgage from John Ridge to John Lucy of lands of Ballynorm, Ballylyotts etc in Co. Roscommon, Aug. 11, 1641. n.782 p.508.

McCausland: PRONI: D. 1550 (Cont'd): Rentals, surveys, etc. of McCausland estates at Limavady, Co. Derry & Carunemore, Shankill Parish, Co. Roscommon, c.1660-1900.

NLI Ms. 10,775: Pakenham-Mahon Papers: Letters etc on valuation & payment of rates out of the estate of Marcus McCausland in the Union of Roscommon, 1848-1851.

Mahon (Baron Hartland): (see also Pakenham Mahon) NLI Ms. 8553; Rentals & miscellaneous documents includes …rentals of estates of Mahon family, Baronets of Castlegar, Co. Galway & Termonbarry, Co. Roscommon, for … the period, 1841-1859.

NLI Ms. 23,022 Mahon Papers: Tenement valuations of estates of Rev. Sir William Ross Mahon 4th Bt., Termonbarry Parish, Co. Roscommon 1 Vol. mid 19th century?

NLI Ms. 23,350-23,351, Mahon papers, farm accounts & rentals of Sir William Vesey Ross Mahon & Sir William Henry Mahon of Castlegar, Co. Galway, 2 large volumes, 1889-1915.

NLI Ms. 18,765: List of freeholders in Strokestown, Co. Roscommon, area registered for Lord Hartland by James & Denis Sweeney; 1815.

NAI M.5596: Petition & orders in Chancery case, 1851, of Richard Irwin & others v. George Knox & others, re estate of Barthomomew Mahon, with refs to Conry family.

NLI Ms. 5,501-5,503, rent ledgers of Baron Hartland, 1803-1818, 1824-1836, part indexed.

NLI Ms. 9,490, Agreements by Maurice Mahon with Tenants & Labourers, 1783-1791

NLI Ms. 10,130, Several Lists of Freeholders c. 30 lists, 1790-1799: 10,130(6), Cordrumman townland; 10,130(9), Barony of Athlone, 26th April 1796; 10,130 (12), Cherryfield & Ardkenna, Kilcooly; & 10,130(14), Tonroe & Kilnamona, Boyle

NLI Ms. 10,152, Rent roll, 1725 (major tenants only) re properties of Nicholas, Thomas & Maurice Mahon (1st Lord Hartland), Robert Sanford & others in County Roscommon,

NLI Ms. 10,152, Rent roll, 1765-68, major tenants only rentals re the properties of Nicholas, Thomas & Maurice Mahon (1st Lord Hartland), Robert Sanford & others in County Roscommon,

NLI Ms. 18,765 List of Freeholders in the Strokestown, Co. Roscommon area, registered for Lord Hartland by James & Denis Sweeney, 1815

NLI Mss. 4001-22, Accounts & rentals (annual), 1842-46, 1850-55, 1861-71, covering townlands in the civil parishes of Ardcarn, Killukin, Killumod.

McDermott: NLI Ms map: Map of estate of Walter J. McDermott in townlands of Castleteheen & Carrowgarve, Co. Roscommon. One folio sheet, 1907. 15 A. 20 (16).

Manners: see St.George

Morris: NLI Ms map: Map of estate of Mary Morris in townland of Ballyglass, Co. Roscommon, 1906. 15 A. 20(17).

Mountrath (Earl of): NLI Ms. 2793: Book of maps of part of estate of Charles Henry, Earl of Mountrath, in Co. Roscommon ….. Folio volume of 35 coloured maps, 1770.

NLI Ms maps: A book of maps of the estate of the earl of Mountrath. By T. Moland, 14 maps of lands in Cos. Roscommon ….1730. n. 3947 p. 3618.

NLI n. 3756 p. 3427 A book of maps (with tenants' names) of part of … Earl of Mountrath's estate … Roscommon: surveyed…1740

Mulligan: NLI Ms map: Map of estate (of J.P. Mulligan?) in townland of Castleteheen, Co. Roscommon. Folio sheet, 1906. 15 A. 20 (18).

Murphy: NLI Ms map: Map of the estate of J.C. Murphy in townlands of Mullen & Reheely, Co. Roscommon, Folio sheet, 1906. 15 A. 20(19).

Nugent: PRONI: Mic. 206: Irish deeds from Stowe Collection re the Nugent family properties in Counties Westmeath, Clare, Longford, Dublin, Roscommon, Wicklow & Queen's Co., 17th c. – 1820. (From the Stowe Collection, San Marino, California Microfilm).

O'Reilly: O'Reilly Mss.: No. 8: Properties & rentals of lands in Cos. Sligo & (Boyle Barony) Roscommon of Myles John O'Reilly, 1849-64. With map of Corderry, Co. Roscommon, surveyed by J. Johnston, in 1821. NLI n. 856 p. 1028

Ormsby: NLI M.10152, Leases c.1803, Grange townland.

NAI M 328a, b: Map of the estate of M.R.W. Ormsby in Callow, Co. Roscommon, by W. Longfield, 1842, Map of same by J. Longfield, 1820.

NAI M. 328 (c,d): Two maps of the estate of M.R.W. Ormsby of lands near Athleague, Co. Roscommon, by John Longfield, 1820.

NAI M.3051: Volume of maps of the estate of Mark R.W. Ormsby in Co. Roscommon, 1820.

O'Rorke: RCBL, Dublin, Miss O'Rorke Collection, Ms. 241, 1889-1930; rentals & accounts re estates of Miss O'Rorke of Taughboy, Co. Donegal & Fuerty, Co. Roscommon, 1 volume

Pakenham Mahon: (see also Mahon) NLI Ms. 10,151: Advertisement for Mahon's Arms, an inn in Strokestown; unattached list of signatures to an address, undated.

NLI Ms. 10,152, Rent roll, 1725, major tenants only;

NLI Ms. 10,154; Rentals & other documents; inc. rentals re properties in Co. Roscommon of various members of the Mahon family, 19th century. There are c. 90 documents.

NLI Ms. 10,146-10,147, notices to quit, 1834, & other miscellaneous estate documents

NLI Ms. 10,130 Thirty-three lists of freeholders in co. Roscommon, c. 1790-1799, some identified as to barony – Athlone, Ballintober, Boyle, Roscommon & Ballimoe

NLI Ms. 10, 129 Documents (2) on Roscommon election expenses, 1806...

Ainsworth (J.F.): Report on Pakenham-Mahon papers (from 1609) ... re the Mahon, Kelly & Sandford families & to lands in Co. Roscommon, (NL rep. on Private Collections, No. 10)

NLI Ms. 10,135 Lists of deeds re Mahon property in Co. Roscommon, early 19th C.

Ms. 10,142 Documents regarding disputed lands of Killeeneravan (Co. Roscommon?), 1781-1797

Ainsworth (J.F.): Report on Pakenham-Mahon papers (from 1609)... now in NLI, re the Mahon, Kelly & Sanford families & lands (NLI Rep. on Private Collections, No. 10).

Ainsworth (J.F.): Supplementary Report on Pakenham-Mahon Papers (from 1703), re lands in Co. Roscommon, (NLI Rep. on Private Collections, No. 280).

Ainsworth (Sir John F.): Supplementary Rept on Pakenham-Mahon Papers mainly correspondence re family & estate matters, some diaries of European tours & accounts, c. 1751-1890. (NLI Rep. on Private Collections, No. 503).

NLI Ms. 10,123 Proposals for a map of Co. Roscommon, 1799

NLI Mss. 10,081-10,110: Letters to family of Mahon of Strokestown, Co. Roscommon, mainly from relations & mainly concerning family & estate affairs, 1720-1858, but inc. refs to ... Strokestown yeomanry, election of 1799, emigration in 1846-1847 etc (c. 1500 pieces).

NLI Ms. 10,150: A request for the appointment of a sanitary committee to deal with fever in Strokestown, undated; circulars of a committee on distress in Ireland, 1822.

NLI D. 12,002-12,089 Eighty-eight deeds re lands in Co. Roscommon of Mahon family of Strokestown, inc. references to Sandford family, with a number of bonds & wills, 1731-1745

NLI D. 12,090-12,206. 117 deeds, mainly re lands in Co. Roscommon of Mahon family of Strokestown, including refs. to Sandford family & a number of bonds & wills, 1750-1775

NLI D. 12,207-12,360. 154 deeds mainly re lands in Roscommon of Mahon family of Strokestown, including refs. to Sandford family & … marriage settlements, bonds & wills, 1776-1799.

NLI Ms. 9486: Account of repairs at Strokestown House, commenced in July, 1843.

NLI n.558 p. 928. Memorandum on the management of the Strokestown estate by John Ross Mahon in his first year as agent for the late Major Mahon, Nov. 8, 1847.

NLI Ms. 9490 Agreements by Maurice Mahon with tenants & labourers, 1783-1791

NLI D. 12,361-12,584. 224 deeds, mainly re lands in Co. Roscommon of Lord Hartland of Strokestown, including a number of bonds & wills, 1800-1815

D. 12,935-13,047. 113 deeds mainly re lands in Co. Roscommon of Henry Sandford Pakenham Mahon, 1826-1894

NLI Ms. 3119: "Photostat" copy of survey of Co. Roscommon transcribed in 1721

NLI D. 12,585-12,934. 350 deeds, mainly re lands in Co. Roscommon of Lord Hartland, of Strokestown, 1816-1825

NLI Ms. D. 11,725-11,868. 144 deeds re lands in Counties Roscommon & Longford, particularly the Strokestown area, of the Mahon family, 1654-1699

NLI Ms. D. 11,869-12,001: 133 deeds relating mainly to lands in Co. Roscommon of the Mahon family of Strokestown, but including also some bonds & wills, 1700-1730

NLI Ms. 10,126, Documents concerning the linen industry in Co. Roscommon, c. 1780-1790

NLI M. 2597, rent ledger with name index, 1795-1804

NLI Ms. 5501-5503, rent ledgers of Baron Hartland, 1803-1818, 1824-1836, part indexed.

NLI Ms.9473, Details of tenants of Maurice Mahon in the baronies of Ballintobber & Roscommon, County Roscommon, c.1817

NLI Ms. 9471, rentals & accounts, 1846-1854; covering townlands in the civil parishes of Bumlin, Cloonfinlough, Elphin, Kilgefin, Kilglass, Kilnamanagh, Kiltrustan, Lisonuffy, Shankill;

NLI Ms. 9472, 1840-1848, rent ledgers of tenants at Kilmacumpsy & Corradrehid, County Roscommon

NLI Ms. 9470, Memorandum book re tenants of the Mahon estate in Termonbarry, Co. Roscommon, 1839-1846

NLI Ms. 9474, Tithe payers on the Strokestown estate, 1838-1839

NLI Ms. 9478; Eight rentals of Mahon estate, Co. Roscommon, early in the mid 19th century

NLI p. 928, Memo on management of Strokestown estate by John Ross Mahon …Nov. 8, 1847

NLI 16 M. 14-16; 101 Coloured maps of Pakenham-Mahon estate in Co. Roscommon, 1734-1895, some with tables of reference, 1734-1895.

NLI Ms. 15,410: Pakenham-Mahon Papers: Miscellaneous documents concerning local government in Co. Roscommon, mainly early 19th c., with a few lists 18th c., including lists of freeholders compiled in connexion with an election.

NLI Ms. 15,411: Pakenham-Mahon Papers: Miscellaneous 19th c. documents, mainly trivial financial documents, concerning the affairs of the Pakenham-Mahon estate, Strokestown, Co. Roscommon.

NLI Ms. 15,372: Pakenham-Mahon Papers: Miscellaneous estimates & accounts concerning tradesmen's supplies & work in repairs to Strokestown House, 1815 (one document), 1843-1845 (for Major Denis Mahon).

NLI Ms.5594: Cash book of the Pakenham-Mahon family, of Co. Roscommon, 1833-1856.

Roberts: London: British Museum: Harleian Ms. 4784: Survey of lands belonging to E. Roberts, … containing plans & descriptions of baronies of … Athlone (Roscommon)…NLI n. 1683 p.1425

St. George: NA London: C. 110 Box 46: Chancery Master's Exhibits. St. George vs. St. George. A large collection of rentals, accounts, letters & other papers re property of Oliver St. George in Roscommon with refs to estate of Thomas Knox of Dungannon & many letters (1723-30) of Owen Gallagher, agent for St. George, 1681-1730, but mostly 1720-30. n. 4540 p. 4406

NLI Ms. 4073: Account book showing allowances & payments to tenants for improvements on a Carrick-on-Shannon estate (Hatley Manor) from 1850. Prepared by Henry T. Darley, 1881.

Charles Manners St George NLI Mss. 4001-22, Accounts & rentals (annual), 1842-46, 1850-55, 1861-71, covering townlands in civil parishes of Ardcarn, Killukin, Killumod.

NLI Mss. 4001-4022: Twenty-two volumes of the estates of Charles St. George in counties Leitrim, Roscommon, Waterford, Tipperary, & Offaly, 1842-1846, 1850-1855, 1861-1871.

Maps of the estate of Richard St. George in Cos Leitrim & Roscommon by R. Frizell & C. Frizell, junior, 1768. NLI n. 3092 p. 2713.

NLI Ms map: Map of the estate of Major St. George French, in electoral division of Cloonyquin & barony of Roscommon…. Folio sheet, 1906. 15 A. 20 (11).

Sanford (See also Mahon): NLI M. 10,152, Rental (major tenants only), 1718; NLI Ms.10152, Leases, c.1750; NLI Ms.10152, Lands to be settled on marriage of Henry Sandford, with tenants' names, 1750; NLI Mss.4281-9, Annual Rentals, 1835-45; covering townlands in the civil parishes of Ballintober, Baslick, Kilkeevin, Boyle, Kiltullagh, Tibohine.

NAI. M. 532: Map by Joseph Boyd of the estate of Henry Sandford in Harystown, Cloonsallagh, Castlerea, Knockroe & Longford, Ballintubber Barony, … 1795.

NAI. M. 540: Map of estate of Henry Sandford in Ardass, Kilkeevan parish, Co. Roscommon, 1781.

NAI Ms. 542a: 542e: Map by M. Egan of part of Lord Mount Sandford's estate in Ballindrimly, Co. Roscommon, 1812. Map of same by A. Higgins, 1760.

NAI Ms. 542b: Map of the estate of Henry Sandford at Malthouse Park, Castlerea, 1785.

RIA Ms. 12 S. 35: Papers (including rentals) of the Mount Sandford estate near Castlereagh, Co. Roscommon, 18th – 19th c.

NAI Ms. 543d: Map to show proposed drainage on the estate of Thomas G.W. Sandford in the Barony of Castlereagh, Roscommon, 19th c.

NLI Mss.4281-4289: Nine rentals of the Castlrea, Emla, Baslick, Buckfield, Miltown, Sallymount, Mullymux, & Ballymore estates of Lord Mount Sandford situate in Cos. Roscommon & Westmeath, 1835-1845.

NLI Ms. 10,152, Rent roll, 1718, major tenants only (on) properties of Robert Sanford & others in County Roscommon

Stafford-King: Rockingham, Boyle – collection of records held at National Library

Styles: Styles family estates in Cos. Roscommon & Donegal. Collection … mainly deeds & rentals of properties of Corlacky & Glenfin, County Donegal, 18th century. (58th Report, p. 21)

Synge: Ms. 2174: Accounts of the estates of Edward Synge, successively bishop of Ferns & Elphin in counties Sligo & Roscommon, 1724-1753.

Ms map: Certified survey of Taughboy, Tishane, etc., in the barony of Athlone, Co. Roscommon, part of the lands of the See of Elphin. Surveyed by James Hanly. Quarto parchment sheet, coloured in outline, 1759. 16 I 13 (1).

Ms map: Part of the lands belonging to the See of Elphin & being in the parish of Kilkerin, barony of Ballintober, Co. Roscommon. By James Hanly. Folio parchment sheet, coloured, Sept. 1741. 16 I 13 (2).

Ms map: A map of Brendrum, Lisserdrea, Ballimore, & Corbally, being the lands of Edward (Synge) Lord Bishop of Elphin, in the parish of Boyle, by James Murray. Folio parchment sheet, couloured in outline, 1742. 16 I. 13(3).

Tenison: NLI Ms. 19,747: Valuation survey of estate of Edward King Tenison in cos. of Roscommon & Tyrone, 1862: 57 coloured maps. (3rd volume of a series).

NLI Ms. 2187: Summary accounts re the estates of Edward King Tenison in counties Sligo, Roscommon & Leitrim, 1844-62, & an abstract of names of purchasers & sums realised by the sale of his estates in Co. Dublin, Nov. 1861.

NLI Ms. 3156: Rent book showing amounts received from tenants of Edward K. Tenison, of Kilronan castle, in Counties Roscommon & Leitrim & Dublin, 1846-1859.

NLI Ms.5101, Rental & Accounts, 1836-40, covering townlands in the civil parishes of Ardcarn, Kilronan. 1836-40. (Thomas Tenison)

Torner: NLI Ms. 15,365: List of burgesses & freemen (of Boyle, Co. Roscommon) compiled June, 1749, in the interest of James Torner, a candidate for .. election.

Tottenham: NAI: Hoey & Denning, parcel 49: Papers re the property of Castletehin alias Castlehine, Co. Roscommon, of Charles Tottenham, 18th-19th c.

Trench: NLI Ms. 9393: Domvile Papers. Memoranda of Papers re the Trench estate in Mayo & Roscommon, made at Heywood (Leix) in 1814.

NLI Ms. 2578: Rental of the Trench estates in Roscommon, 1840-79.

Trimlestown: NAI. Hoey & Denning, parcel 50: Papers re sale of estate of Lord Trimlestown in Runnabacken, Co. Roscommon, 1906.

Westby: GO 178, pp. 407-12: Pedigree of Westby of …. Strokestown, Co. Roscommon, of High Park, …, c. 1690-1859.

White, Robert: NLI Ms. 8841, 1837-1842, Misc documents, 1837-1842 inc rentals re lands at Arigna, Co. Roscommon

Whyte: NLI Mss. 4023-4044; 1874-1896; Rentals & accounts of the estates of Mrs. Petronella Whyte in Counties Longford & Roscommon, 1873-1896, 22 volumes

Wills: NAI M. 545: Maps & plans re the property of the Wills family in Co. Roscommon, 1722, 1760, 1769, 1807,and n.d.

NAI M. 545 a-b: Survey of 14 maps of the estate of R.W. Wills in Co. Roscommon by M. Egan, 1807. Map of house & demesne of Wilsgrove.

NAI M. 544g: Map of part of the Wills estate in Ballinlough.., by M. Kane, 1880.

NAI M. 544d, h: Map of part of Longford, Co. Roscommon, n.d. Protractions of A.W. Young's farm at Longford, Co. Roscommon by M. Leech, 1850.

Additional Estate Manuscript Sources for County Roscommon
The following are some manuscripts re estates where no landlord name is provided. They include records from the Land League and the Land Commission.

NLI Ms. 17,711 Land League Papers, 22 returns listing leases, rents & fines by member of Irish National Land Leagues, mainly in Roscommon & Tipperary branches 1850-1880

NLI Ms. 17,706, Land League, Mayo, Roscommon, Tipperary, 50 monthly branch reports, proceedings, subscriptions, evictions in 4 folders, March 1880-March 1881

NLI Ms. 17710, Land League papers, 35 files, applications for legal costs, correspondence between tenants, solicitors & League, 7 folders, 1881

NLI Ms. 26,188 Estates, Joseph Brennan Papers, miscellaneous official papers

NLI Ms. 17,714, Land League Papers, 100 evictions, form completed for Ladies National Land League … Roscommon … particulars of tenants families, rents, landlords, 1881

Index to the townland survey of County of Roscommon, with manuscript notes on the divisions of districts, 1837-9. NLI 16 K. 16 (23).

NLI Ms. 2016: Manuscript field book for the Roscommon survey, with notes & Plans of roads in Co. Roscommon, 1813-16 & notes & plans of survey of grounds in South County Dublin, 1804. By William Edgeworth.

NLI Ms. 3242: Manuscript field book for the Roscommon survey, containing plans of roads in Co. Roscommon by William Hampton, land surveyor 1813.

Manuscript map: A survey of the Lough Gara district, situated chiefly in the County Roscommon done by the order of the Commissioners of the bogs, by J. Longfield. Three sheets, coloured, 1811. NLI 16 D. 16.

NAI M. 536: Map of river dividing Aneenaghara & Clonee estates. 1834.

NAI M. 542d: Map of holding in Lisliddy, Lisboy & Emlagh, by Richard Beytagh, n.d.

Manuscript map: Baronies of Athlone, Moycarn, & part of Ballintobber. A composite map representing the original Ordnance Survey of 1837 & the Stafford Survey, 1636. Drawn by Robert Johnston, (Folio sheets, 28-29, 35-36), 1956. NLI 20 D.

NLI Mss. 1543-7: A collection of materials copied from various printed sources re the history of Athlone & the surrounding area, 1690-1899, compiled by Malachy Moran between 1910 &1935. With a volume of indexes.

Manuscript maps: Maps of lands in the baronies of Boyle, Castlereagh, & Frenchpark, Co. Roscommon. 39 maps, 1741-1829. NLI 21 F. 44 (40-78).

Maps of …Athlone, Ballintober, Ballymoe & Boyle. 1755-1836. NLI 21 F. 43 (1-39).

Maps of lands in the baronies of Frenchpark, Moycarn, & Roscommon, 39 maps, 1716-1838. NLI 21 F. 45 (79-116).

Maps of lands in the baronies of Boyle, Castlereagh & Frenchpark, Co. Roscommon. By John Brownrigg, John Longfield & others. 39 maps, 1741-1829. NLI 21 F. 44 (40-78).

NAI. M. 544c: Map of Ballyglass Dodwell, Co. Roscommon, 1831.

NAI M. 542b: Map of holdings in Ballinlough, Co. Roscommon, n.d.

NAI M. 542c: Map of the boundaries of the estates of Lord Mount Sandford & Lord de Freyne at Castlerea & Frenchpark, n.d.

NAI M. 542d: Map of holdings in Lisliddy, Lisboy & Emlagh, Co. Roscommon, n.d.

NAI M. 543c: Maps of Ballinlough drainage district, Co. Roscommon, 1880.

NAI 544i: Maps of roads from Castlerea to Swinford & Castlerea to Ballinlough 1846.

NAI M. 545c: Map of lands in parish of Kilkeevin, Ballintubber .. 1722.

Plan & survey of lands of Twomore (Toomore), Mullagnashee, Knocknagauna, etc., Co. Roscommon. Large folio sheet., 18th c. NLI 16 I .14(1).

Certified survey of lands of Carrowmore, Co. Roscommon Sept., 1738. NLI 16 I. 14 (3).

Map & survey of Kiltobranks…Crevey & Kiltimaine… 1788. NLI 16 I. 14 (5).

A map of Ballagh, Co. Roscommon, Oct., 1716. NLI 16 I. 14 (10).

NAI Ms. 1063: River Boyle Navigation loan debentures, 1799-1800.

NAI M. 544b: Plan of site for intended court house at Castlerea, Co. Roscommon, by Michael Betagh, 1844.

NAI Ms. 531: Map of the Brewery plot, Castlerea, Co. Roscommon, 1827.

NAI M. 544e: Map of Churchboro, Co. Roscommon, 1830.

NAI M.534-5: Maps ..of lands in Cloonagh, Lecarrow, etc., Co. Roscommon, 1717.

Plan & survey of .. Twomore (Toomore), Mullagnashee, Knocknagauna etc., Co. Roscommon. Large folio sheet, 18th c. NLI 16 I. 14(1).

NAI M.542e: Map of holdings of Toureagh, Co. Roscommon, n.d.

NAI M.6887: Map of Tarmon of Kilronan, Co. Roscommon, 1821.

NLI Ms. 7549: Larcom Papers: Letters to Larcom & memoranda on the destruction of Rooskey Bridge, Co. Roscommon, 1844.

PRONI Mic. 206 add.: Stowe Collection: Deeds for properties in Counties …Roscommon, … c. 1670-c.1819. (Microfilm).

San Marino: Henry E. Huntington Library: Stowe papers: 32 deeds from Stowe Papers re lands in .. Roscommon, various dates, early 17th – early 19th c. NLI n.5853 p. 6071.

Oxfordshire Record Office: Maps & plans of Castlerea & Ballaghadereen Railway, 19th c.

Killtulagh, Tuam Diocese: Diocesan Archives: Half-yearly rental of See of Killala & Achrony, 1716-17. Ecclesiatical report for Dioceses of Killala & Achrony, 1830. Return of benefices in same, 1835. Licence for non-residence of Rev. R Falkiner, rectory of Kiltulagh, Co. Roscommon, 1825. NLI n.5297 p.5406

RIA: Ms. 24 Q. 35: 20 deeds re lands in Dublin & Roscommon, 1673, 1717, 1812.

Ordnance Survey Office: John O'Donovan name books of Co. Roscommon, 19th c. NLI n.553-4 p.924-5.

Ordnance Survey Office: Manuscript index of all names on the first 6 inch survey maps, Co. Roscommon, 19th c. NLI n.4633 p.4623.

RIA Mss. 14 F. 8-9: Ordnance Survey letters to Co. Roscommon, 1837.

RIA: Ordnance Survey memoirs. Box 50, .. Roscommon... NLI n.3167 p.2787

Manchester: John Rylands Library: Irish Ms. 113: Extracts from D.H. Kelly from the Ordnance Survey papers in the RIA re Co. Roscommon, c.1865. NLI n.3538 p.3156.

NLI Ms. 1549: Transcripts from Tithe Applotment Books re various parishes in the counties of .. Roscommon, & Galway, made by Malachy Moran, 19-

NLI D. 7915-7955: 41 deeds re property in Cos. … Roscommon, including refs to families of Cotes, Kearney, Maher, Reynolds, & Clarke, with some wills, mainly 19th c.

NAI M. 1079: Portfolio of maps by P.J. Lynam of various townlands in Cos. Mayo, Roscommon & Galway, 1885-8.

RIA Ms. 24 E. 35: A collection of about 30 deeds re lands in Roscommon, 1812, & in Dublin, 1673 &1717.

Chapter 9   Grave Records and Inscriptions

Few Irish churches kept burial records so gravestones and associated memorial records are one of the few pre-1864 sources of information about date and place of death.   Most provide only basic details i.e. the name of the deceased and the date of death. However, some provide valuable information about relationships. The graves of poorer persons were often unmarked, as gravestones could not be afforded by their surviving relatives, or were marked with wooden materials which have now rotted away. In some areas the stone used for gravestones has also worn so that the inscription is no longer legible.

It was not uncommon for Roman Catholics, Methodists, and Presbyterians to be buried in Church of Ireland graveyards. Until the early 19th century there was a legal requirement that graveyards were the property of the Established Church, and that the minister was entitled to a fee for burials, although this law was often not imposed. Church of Ireland graveyards should always be checked no matter the religious denomination of the family.

A notable group involved in gravestone transcription was the Association for the Preservation of the Memorials of the Dead (1888-1921) whose supporters transcribed records from hundreds of sites. These were published in the Association's Journal (JAPMD) but are selective, since they were generally dependent on contributions by individual members.[18]   Extracts of memorials from all over the island were published though not on any systematic basis. The stated purpose was to 'secure a record of existing tombs and monuments of interest', and some transcribers showed a regrettable elitist bias.[19]

In visiting and exploring graveyards, it is important to leave a site in the same or better condition as one found it. A booklet on *The Care and Conservation of Graveyards* is available on the Co. Roscommon website - www.roscommoncoco.ie/burialgrounds/. A survey of 287 Burial Grounds in the county is also available in this website, and includes:

o **77 Children's burial grounds** The custom of separate burial of small children was common practice from early medieval times until fairly recently.

o **23 Church of Ireland burial grounds** - many attached to churches.

o **1 Quaker burial ground** - There is one Quaker graveyard at Killea, Knockcroghery.

o **186 Roman Catholic burial grounds**

Local genealogical and historical societies have also transcribed and published complete surveys of graveyards, usually in local journals. Roscommon Heritage & Genealogical Company (RHGC) has also indexed some graveyards. The following are the parishes for which records are available, and their location.

Aughrim (Old): Roscommon Heritage and Genealogical Society, RHGC.

Bumlin: Killinordin RHGC,

Cam: IGRS Collection (138 inscriptions), GO. Also Gacquin, William, *Tombstone inscriptions in Cam Old Cemetery*, Cam Cemetery Committee, Cam, 1992, NLI, Ir 941 p 120(1): also Tombstone Inscriptions Vol II (Pub. IGRS) page 1235

Cloonfinlough : Ballintemple, RHGC,

Cloontuskert: IGRS Collection, GO,

Dysart: RHGC. Also IGRS Collection (103 inscriptions), GO

Dysert: Old Tombstone Inscriptions Vol II (Pub. IGRS) page 1252

Elphin: Elphin Cathedral, C of I, GO Ms 622 p. 151, GO,

Fuerty: RHGC,

Jamestown: GO Ms. 622, 170.

Kilteevan Parish Gravestone Inscriptions, 1864-1900, An Index to Kilteevan Cemetery,

Kiltrustan: RHGC,

Kilverdin: RHGS

Lissonuffy: RHGC,

Roscommon: Hill St., C of I, GO. Ms. 622, p. 170. Also RHGC
St. Peter's: Athlone, King Street, C of I, Pos. 5309 (with parish
    registers), NLI,
Strokestown: RHGS, also GO Ms. 622, 174, and 182.
Taghboy: see Jamestown above
Taghmaconnell: C of I, IGRS Collection (71 inscriptions), GO.
Taughmaconnell, Old. Tombstone Inscriptions Vol II (Pub. IGRS)
    pp.1266 & 1274
Tisrara: Mount Talbot (Tisrara), C of I, IGRS Collection (144
    inscriptions), GO; also Tombstone Inscriptions Vol II (Pub.
    IGRS) page 1283
Tisrara: Carrowntemple, Higgins, Jim, *The Tisrara medieval church*
    Carrowntemple [...],Tisrara Heritage [...] Committee, Four
    Roads, 1995, NLI, Ir 7941 h 25
Lastly, but by no means least, cemeteries and graveyards in countries
where people of Roscommon emigrated should also be researched.
One excellent example is an interesting book covering a multitude of
people from Roscommon and other Irish counties is R. Andrew Pierce's
The Stones Speak; Irish Place Names from Inscriptions in Boston's
Mount Calvary Cemetery, published by the New England Historic and
Genealogical Society, Boston, in 2000. The following is one recorded
entry.

    1250.   Bridget **MORGAN**,
            Died Nov. 13, 1882 Aged 61 years.
            Erected by her husband Patrick
            Natives of parish Cam Co. Roscommon Ireland
            Their children
            John born June 27, 1849 Died Dec. 19 1850
            Richard [?] Born Nov. 8 1853, died Nov. 24 1854
            Patrick Jr. Born August 13 1861 Died Oct 14, 1862
            Anne Died Dec 6, 1888, Aged 29 yrs
            Patrick Morgan Died April 13 1894 Aged 75 yrs
            Mary E. **GATELY** Died Sept 8, 1901 Aged 41 Yrs[20]

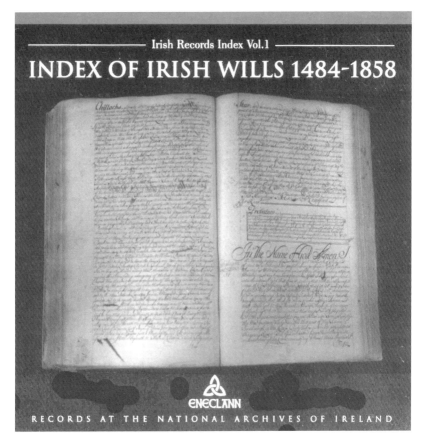

*An index of testamentary records held at the National Archives for the
period 1484-1858 published on CD by Eneclann (1999)
www.eneclann.ie*

Chapter 10   Wills, Administrations and Marriage Records

A **Will** is a written communication by a person as to how their property (estate) should be disposed of after their death. An **Administration** is the decision of the Probate Court on the distribution of the property of a deceased person who dies without making a will. Wills or testamentary records are very important documents which can provide valuable information for determining family relationships, social status and also biographical details. To understand wills, and the process of administration of wills, it is necessary to know some of the terminology. Some brief definitions are:

Testator: the writer of a will.
Executor: A person nominated by the testator to carry out the testator's instructions.
Intestate: If a person dies without leaving a valid will, they die 'intestate.' The Probate court then decides on the distribution ot the deceased person's property.
Administrator: The party appointed by the court to dispose of the property described in the administration, usually either a relative of the deceased or an attorney.
Administration Bond: An administrator usually enters a bond for a certain amount of money as an assurance that they will execute the administration as instructed.
Probate: The process by which a court declares a will to be legally valid and appoints an executor or administrator to carry out the instructions in the will.

The reader should note that Chapter 15 also contains many references to Roscommon family wills, administrations, and marriage records. Unfortunately, the major collection of Irish wills was destroyed in the Public Records Office fire in 1922. The probate records still available to genealogists are as follows:

Original Wills and Administrations – these often contain useful information on family relationships as individual beneficiaries, executors of witnesses will usually be described by reference to the deceased. e.g. " …to my cousin William Murphy, I leave…"

Will Abstracts – For both legal and genealogical reasons, details of persons and properties in certain wills have been abstracted and either published, or made available in manuscript form.

Will Indexes – Although the main will collections are destroyed, the indexes to the collection have survived. These provide name, residence and date of death of the testator.

As noted earlier, the Church of Ireland was the body responsible for administering the probate system until 1858, when this responsibility was passed to the Probate courts. This date is therefore an important one in searching probate records.

Pre-1858 Wills and Administrations: Before 1858, each Church of Ireland diocese maintained its own probate court which was called a Diocesan or Consistorial Court. Wills from County Roscommon may therefore be found in will indexes from the Consistorial courts of Achrony, Ardagh, Clonfert, Elphin or Tuam. If the deceased left an estate worth greater than five pounds in a second diocese then probate was granted by a higher court, which was the Prerogative Court of Armagh. Such wills were generally made by wealthy individuals, but landowners of property which straddled the border of two or more dioceses may also fall under the probate jurisdiction of the Prerogative Court of Armagh.

Post-1858 Wills and Administrations: With the disestablishment of the Ecclesiastical Courts (Prerogative and Diocesan) in 1857, a civil court system was introduced. Under the Court of Probate and Letters of Administration Act (Ireland) of 1857, eleven District Registries were created to prove wills and grant administrations. All of County Roscommon is located in the Probate District of Tuam. In addition, a Principal Registry was created and effectively replaced the Prerogative Court by ruling on cases where the testator had property in more than one District Registry.

Surviving Pre 1858 Records of Prerogative Court: There are several types of records:

Prerogative Will Books: None of the original Prerogative Wills survived the 1922 fire, however some will books (books into which original wills were transcribed) survived for the following years: 1664-1684; 1706-1708; 1726-1729; 1777 (surnames beginning A-L only); 1813 (surnames beginning with K-Z only); 1834 (surnames beginning A to E only). These are located in the NAI and are indexed in their testamentary card index.

Abstracts and Sketch Pedigrees: Sir William Betham recorded family relationships from a large collection of pre-1800 Prerogative Wills and Administrations before their destruction in 1922. These records, commonly known as the Betham Abstracts, are held at the NAI. The GO in the NLI also holds sketch pedigrees crafted by Betham based on these abstracts. The Society of Genealogists in London also holds copies.

362   *Index to Prerogative Wills of Ireland.*

1740 **Ormsby**, Frances, Dublin, widow	1763 **Ormsby**, Wm., Naas, co. Kildare, gent.
1751 ,, Francis, Willybrook, co. Sligo, esq.	1784 ,, Wm., Castledargan, co. Sligo, esq.
1680 ,, George, Loughmask, co. Mayo, esq.	1791 ,, William, Dublin, gent.
1749 ,, George, Tobervaddy, co. Roscommon, esq.	1805 ,, William, Dublin city, esq. [See HORNSBY.]
1757 ,, George, Dublin	1662 **Ormsbye**, lieut. Thos., Comyn, co. Sligo, esq.
1788 ,, George, Robsgrove, co. Roscommon, esq.	1802 **Ormston**, Jean (Copy)
1799 ,, Gilbert, Athlone, co. Westmeath	1782 **O'Rorke**, Andrew, Creevy, co. Leitrim, gent.
1758 ,, Hannah, Cummin, co. Sligo, widow	1761 ,, Farrell, Carrow Crum
1694 ,, Henry, Rathlee, co. Sligo, esq.	1790 ,, Hugh, Creevagh, co. Sligo, esq.
1809 ,, James	1783 ,, Hyacinth, Ballycurry, co. Sligo, esq.
1694 ,, dame Jane, Richmond, Surrey, widow (Copy)	1797 ,, Mary, Toome, co. Antrim, wid.
1714 ,, Jane, Belanamore, co. Mayo, widow	1809 **O'Rourke**, Fras., Carrowerin, co. Leitrim, gent.
1755 ,, Jane, Dublin, widow	1781 ,, Hugh, Creevagh, co. Sligo.
1634 ,, John, Armagh, gent.	1794 **Orpen**, George
1711 ,, John, Alaca, co. Limerick, esq.	1740 ,, Richd., Ardtully, co. Kerry, gt.
1721 ,, John, Dublin, esq. [esq.	1770 ,, Richard, Valentia, co. Kerry
1727 ,, John, Athlacca, co. Limerick,	1810 ,, Richard, Ardtully, co. Kerry, esq.
1745 ,, John, Cloghan, co. Mayo, esq.	1768 ,, Thos., Killowen, co. Kerry, clk.
1799 ,, John, Cummin, co. Sligo, esq.	1805 **Orpin**, Fras., Douglass, Cork city, clk.
1808 ,, John, Gortudrabby, co. Mayo	1722 ,, John, Dublin, gent.
1734 ,, Lettice, Dublin, spinster	1752 ,, John, Dublin, glazier
1754 ,, Lewis, Tobervaddy, co. Roscommon, esq.	1727 ,, Thos., Carrickfergus, glazier
1681 ,, Mary, spinster	1739 **Orr**, Alex., Belfast, co. Antrim, mct.

Extract from 'Index to the Prerogative Wills of Ireland 1536-1810' in Dublin in 1897 & republished by Genealogical Publishing Co. in 1989.

Prerogative Will Indexes: The indexes to Prerogative Wills do survive and are arranged alphabetically by surname providing testator's address, occupation and year of probate. The NAI hold the original manuscript index for the years 1536-1857.

Sir Arthur Vicars compiled an index for the period 1536 to 1810 which was published as an *Index to the Prerogative Wills of Ireland 1536-1810* in Dublin in 1897 & republished by Genealogical Publishing Co. in 1989.

Irish Wills in Prerogative Court of Canterbury: The NLI holds an Index to the Abstracts of Wills of Irish Testators registered in the Prerogative Court of Canterbury 1636-1698 which is available in the Manuscript Reading Room. These are relevant for Irish people who had property in England.

Prerogative Administration Grant Books: All original grants or Letters of Administration were destroyed in the 1922 fire and only a few Grant Books (books into which original grants were transcribed) survived. These are as follows: 1684-1688, 1748-1751; 1839. Also the Prerogative Day Books for the years 1784-1788. These are held at the NAI.

Prerogative Grant Indexes: This is a combined index of Prerogative Grants of Administrations, Probate of Wills and Marriage Licences for the years 1595 to 1858. This is arranged alphabetically under initial letter of surname, listing name, address, occupation, condition year and nature of grant. This is available in the NAI.

> **732** DOGHERTY, JAMES, Tully, Co. Roscommon, gent.
>   29 Jan. 1743. Précis, ½ p., 26 Aug. 1745.
>   James Lawder the younger, Lowfield, Co. Roscommon, Esq. Exors.:
> John Harward, Portorny, Co. Roscommon, Esq., Wentworth Thewles, Dublin, gent., and Edmond Kelly, Churchborough, Co. Roscommon, gent.
>   His estate of Tully, B. Bal[l]intober, parish of Kilmore, Co. Roscommon.
>   Witnesses : George Cammell, Hugh Purcell, Owen Mulvey, all of Churchborough, Co. Roscommon, yeoman.
>   Memorial witnessed by : Owen Mulvey, John Lawder, Dublin, gent.
> 120, 153, 82180   James Lawder (seal)

Entry from 'Registry of Deeds, Dublin: Abstracts of Wills' Vol.1 edited by P.B. Eustace and others

Registry of Deeds: As wills are often important in proving title to property, a good number of wills were registered at the Registry of Deeds. The IMC has published abstracts in the three volumes of *Registry of Deeds, Dublin: Abstracts of Wills* edited by P.B. Eustace and others. Volume I covers 1708 to 1745. Volume II covers 1746 to 1785, and Volume III, (edited by P.B. Eustace and Eilish Ellis) (pub.1984) covers 1785-1832.(see p.86)

Surviving Pre-1858 Material of the Diocesan Courts of Roscommon:

Achrony: Fragments of Wills & Administration bonds from Achonry Diocese. NAI pos. 1727

Ardagh & Clonmacnoise: Index to Ardagh Wills to 1857 are published in a Supplement to the *Irish Ancestor* 1971

Clonfert: These include:
Indexes to Clonfert Wills (1663-1857), Administration Bonds (1771-1857) and Marriage License Bonds are published in *Irish Ancestor* 1970.
NAI Index to diocesan wills, Diocese of Cashel and Emly, 1618-1858; Clogher, 1661-1858; Clonfert, 1663-1857; Cloyne, 1621-1858. n. 1723 p. 1723-4

Elphin
Fragments of Wills & Administration bonds: Wills 1650-1858; 1601-1858 (fragments); 1603-1838 (Surnames F-V); 1615-1842 (unproved, W only): & Administration Bonds: 1726-1848 1765-1833. NAI pos. 1727
Wills & Deeds from Co. Sligo, 1605-32, NLI Ms. 2164
NAI Index to diocesan wills, Diocese of Dromore, 1678-1858; Elphin, 1650-1858; Killala and Achrony fragments only; Kilmore, 1682-1857; Leighlin, 1682-1857. NAI n. 1727 p. 1727

Tuam
Fragments of Wills & Administration bonds: Wills 1648-1858 (damaged); Administration Bonds 1692-1857
NAI Will books containing copies of wills registered in Tuam Registry, 1858-1901, reference number n. 1831-2 NAI p. 1831-2

GO 707, abstracts, mainly re wills mentioning Burke families in the Diocese of Tuam 1784-1820

County Roscommon
NAI R.C. 5/29-31: Transcripts of deeds and wills recited in Chancery Inquisitions for the Counties Galway, Mayo, Roscommon and Sligo, with an index for all counties.

Testamentary Card Index: If an entry from the above listed indexes is located, the Testamentary card index at the NAI may be consulted to determine if that particular Administration or Will survives. This NAI index encompasses all surviving pre-1858 and post-1858 testamentary sources (except the surviving post-1858 probate district will books). Bethams's abstracts and other abstract collections are indexed separately to the main NAI testamentary card index.

Yearly Calendars of Wills and Administrations: The NAI also holds yearly 'Calendars' of Wills which begin in 1858. Essentially, these are abstracts of wills from 1858 onwards and are printed in large bound volumes which provide researchers with the deceased's name, address, date of death, place of death, occupation, and value of estate. The date and place of probate or administration and the grantee's name, address, and relationship to the deceased is also provided. When an entry of interest is identified, the testamentary card index or surviving will book should then be consulted. Copies of the original wills can be ordered at the NAI and be posted out to the researcher.

A Guide to Copies and Abstracts of Irish Wills: Rev. Wallace Clare compiled *A Guide to Copies and Abstracts of Irish Wills*, Sharman, 1930, which is arranged by name, address, date of probate and reference to one of the following categories: a) copies and extracts of Irish wills held by the Society of Genealogists in London; b) copies of wills in the Prerogative will books which survived the 1922 Four Courts fire; c) early original wills held in English archives, and; d) copies and extracts of wills published in some historical and genealogical magazines and journals, family histories, etc.

Index of Irish Wills 1484-1858* and *Index to the Prerogative Wills of Ireland, 1536-1810, & Supplement: Eneclann's *Index of Irish Wills 1484-1858* is helpful in locating references to wills across Ireland and should not be overlooked in conducting research. Archive CD Books

Ireland, an affiliate of Eneclann, has also recently released the *Index to the Prerogative Wills of Ireland, 1536-1810, & Supplement*. The *Index to the Prerogative Wills of Ireland, 1536-1810, & Supplement* lists 321 individuals with County Roscommon addresses out of an index of 40,000 Irish wills. This index gives the name of every person who left a will, their address, rank or occupation and the date of probate. This index was compiled by Sir Arthur Vicars who based his work on the abstracts of the original wills compiled by Sir William Betham, and is the only index to his voluminous collections of abstracts and extracts in existence.

Index to Will Abstracts in the Genealogical Office: The GO holds an index of will abstracts which is arranges alphabetically by surname giving forename, address, occupation, date and reference to the collection. This was published in *Analecta Hibernica* Volume 17, pp. 151-348.

Wills at the Irish Land Commission: Chapter 7 references an index to wills (mainly 19th century) which is available at the Irish Land Commission.

Banns and Marriage Licences: Churches had two methods for ensuring that there were no impediments to a marriage. The first was the reading or posting of 'Banns' which is an announcement of a couple's intention to marry. The Banns effectively provided three weeks public notice of the upcoming marriage so that objections could be made. The Banns were read in the parish church of both the prospective bride and groom and also in the church where the marriage was going to take place. Interestingly, Banns were considered as a badge of poverty by some in society and were thus not the favourite avenue for many couples. Banns could be waived if the Church of Ireland minister was paid a fee.

The second method used by the Established Church (prior to 1858) was the Marriage Licence. Marriage Licence Bonds involved a payment which was essentially a surety to indemnify the church against damages that may be sought if there was an unexpected marriage impediment. Two types of marriage licences could be issued:
o   Diocesan Marriage Licence Bonds – valid for three months and allowed the couple to marry immediately.

o   Prerogative Marriage Licence Bonds – issued by the Prerogative
     Court of Armagh and permitted the couple to marry anywhere they
     wished without time restrictions.

Indexes to Marriage Licence Bonds: Prerogative Marriage Licence
Bond Indexes:
o   1750-1861 NAI (alphabetically arranged by surname)
o   1629-1858 GO Ms. 605-607

Diocesan Marriage Licences & Bonds Indexes

NAI Indexes to marriage licence bonds for the Dioceses of Killaloe,
1719-1845, Clonfert, 1739 and 1815-44, Limerick, 1827-44, Ardfert,
1820-and 1835. NAI n. 1882 p. 1882

NAI Index to diocesan administration bonds, Diocese of Clonfert,
Killala and Achrony, Limerick, Ardfert, 1738-1837. n. 1729 p. 1729

NAI Betham Mss.: Indexes compiled by Sir William Betham of wills,
administrations and marriage licences of the dioceses of Waterford,
Elphin, Cloyne, and Kilmore, c. 1660-1837. n. 1784 p. 1784

NAI Index to diocesan administration bonds, Dioceses of Dublin and
Kildare, 1697-1848; Elphin, 1726-1857; Ferns, 1765-1833; Killaloe,
1704-1857; Kilmore, 1728-1857

NAI Indexes to marriage license bonds for Kildare Diocese, 1790-
1865; Elphin Diocese, 1753-1845 and Killala and Achrony Diocese,
1787-1842 n. 1881 p. 1881

Chapter 11   Directories and Occupational Sources

Occupational and service records can contain valuable information on dates and places of birth and places of residence.[21] However, for most common occupations, few primary source records are available. The evidence of tenant farmers, agricultural or industrial workers, shopkeeper employees, etc. prior to 1901 is unfortunately poor. However, those in the military or in professions such as the clergy, the police, legal or medical fields are often well documented.

Commercial and Social directories were the early forebears of the 'Yellow Pages', in that they listed tradesmen, professionals, public officials and often the gentry within a town or region. They are therefore a source for finding ancestors who ran businesses in towns or villages as clothiers, shoemakers, grocers, clergy, lawyers or teachers. Ancestors may also be listed if they were affluent land owners or wealthy farmers. Roscommon commercial and social directories exist for towns such as Boyle, Castlerea, Roscommon or Strokestown. These are available in the NLI, and on microfilm in the NAI.

1824 J. Pigot and Co., *City of Dublin and Hibernian Provincial Directory* includes traders, nobility, gentry, and clergy lists of **Boyle, Castlerea, Elphin, Roscommon, and Strokestown** (see p.92).

1846 Slater's, *National Commercial Directory of Ireland* lists nobility, clergy, traders, etc. in **Boyle, Castlerea, Elphin, Roscommon, and Stokestown**.s

1856 Slater's, *Royal National Commercial Directory of Ireland* lists nobility, gentry, clergy, traders, etc., in **Boyle, Castlerea, Elphin, Roscommon, and Stokestown**.

1870 Slater's, *Directory of Ireland* contains trade, nobility, and clergy lists for **Boyle, Castlrea, Elphin, Roscommon, and Strokestown**.

Directory.   **CASTLEBAR.**   **Connaught.**

PUBLICANS·
Dunn Michael, Market-street
Flanaly Peter, Market-street
Herron Thomas, Market-street
Malony Michael, Market-street
Morgan Edward, Market-street
Murphy Roger, Market-street
Sherridan Martin, Market-street
Walsh Anthony, Market-street
Walsh Sarah, Market-streeet

SADDLERS AND HARNESS MAKERS·
Fair Campbell, Market-street
Morris Richard, Market-street

TAILORS·
Burke Thomas, Narrow-lane
Garan Martin, Thomas-street

Hill John, Green
Nelson John, Market-street
Ryan Patrick, Shamble-street

TALLOW CHANDLERS.
Dudgeon John, Market-street
Hynes Levy, Market-street
Tiernou Mary, Market-street

WATCH MAKER·
Topham Edward, Market-street

WINE AND SPIRIT MERCHANTS·
Goulding Thomas, Market-stree
Young Thomas, Market-street

Miscellaneous
Burns James, butter dealer, Mar-
ket-street
Young Mary, stationer

EXCISE OFFICE·
Charles O'Malley, esq. collector
Alexander Bell, gent. pro-collector

STAMP OFFICE·
Francis Henry Wright, esq. distri-
butor for the county

COACHES &c·
A branch of the Galway Mail passes from
Westport every morning at five for
Ballinasloe, and, returning for West-
port, calls every evening at eight, at
the office, Market-street.

Goods may be conveyed to Dublin and
other places by hired Cars.

CASTLEREA,

IN the county of Roscommon, is a considerable market and post town, situated 84 miles west north west of Dublin, 14 north west of Roscommon, 14 south of Boyle, and 14 west of Strokestown. It is the property of Lord Henry Sandford, at present a minor. This nobleman's domain and mansion are extremely interesting, the park is well planted with wood, and the river Suck runs through its centre, passing immediately before the windows of the castle. Indeed the whole neighbourhood is thickly strewed with beautiful seats. Here are the remains of an ancient bridge, well worth the notice of the antiquarian. The public buildings are a neat Gothic church ; a chapel ; and a dispensary, supported by subscription. There are also extensive bleach grounds ; and the flax mills, under the patronage of the Sandford family, are a great benefit to the neighbouring peasantry, as a very small sum only is charged for breaking and dressing the material. A market is held on Wednesday for butter and oats, and another on Saturday for cattle and provisions. The three fairs are on the 23rd of May, the 21st of June, and the 7th of November. The population amounts to 1940.

POST OFFICE.—*Post Mistress,* Miss Bell. The Dublin mail is despatched by horse at six in the morning to Roscommon, and returns at three in the afternoon.

NOBILITY, GENTRY AND CLERGY.

Balfe James, esq. Runnimead
Balfe John, esq. Clonalis
Balfe Michael, esq. South-park
Balfe Nicholas, esq. Heathfield
Blundell Rev. William, Glebe
Dillon Charles, esq.
French Christr. esq. Frenchlawn

Gray ——, Captain, Westmeath
  militia, Dalefield
Lloyd William, esq.
Lyons Thomas, esq.
Magrath Thomas, esq.
M'Dermott Rev. Henry, P. P. Arm
O'Connor Eccles Daniel, esq.
O'Connor Daniel, esq.

Sandford Lord Henry, Castle
Smith Patrick, esq.
Stones Rev. ——, Ballinlough
Tighe Patrick, esq. Fort-William
Tobyn Michael, esq.
Wills Robert, esq. Willsgrove
Young Owen, esq. magistrate, Har-
  ristown

MERCHANTS, TRADESMEN, &c.

PROFESSIONAL GENTLEMEN.
Campbell Arthur, M. D.
Kelly Edmund, apothecary.
Kelly Luke, surgeon
Nathan Charles, apothecary
Wild Thos. M. D.

BAKERS
Corcoran James
Darcy Martin
Hynes Henry
Mitchell Luke

BOOT AND SHOE MAKERS·
Clarke Thomas
Dunn Robert
Hawthorn George
Hipwell George
Kelly Patrick
King John
Lynch Timothy
Swanwick John

CARPENTERS & COACH MAKERS·
Doulan John
Ingriam Arthur
Mannion Michael
M'Laughlin William
Tullis Daniel

GROCERS.
Brodrick Michael

Burke John
Coffee John
Cotton Cox
Dillon Thomas
Feagan Edward
Flynn John
Flynn Patrick
Fitzgibbons Edward
Fitzgibbons William
Foley John
Fox Joseph
Gormly Patrick
Hynnes Michael
M'Dermott Owen
M'Dermott Patrick
Morris Patrick
Morris William

HATTERS·
Dillon Thomas
Murphy Edmund

INNKEEPERS.
Fenny Daniel
Gibbons Thomas

LINEN AND WOOLLEN DRAPERS·
Carter Catherine
Donohoe John
Fitzgibbons Edward
Fitzgibbons Michael

Fitzgibbons William
Kelly Patrick
Morris James

PUBLICANS.
Berny William
Beytash Patrick
Dunn James
Flood Peter
Gannon Owen
Giblon Michael
Handbury Owen
Mahon Oliver
Mitchell John
Moffatt Martin

SMITHS AND NAILORS
Blackburn Thomas
Gormly William
M'Cormack James
Moran James
Mulheran Roderick

TAILORS.
Carney Patrick
Hynnes George
Keane Robert

TALLOW CHANDLERS·
Daly Robert
Gallagher George

C c   120

Sample page from Pigott's City of Dublin and Hibernian Provincial Directory 1824.

1881 Slater's, *Royal National Commercial Directory of Ireland* lists traders, clergy, nobility & farmers in and around **Boyle, Castlerea, Elphin, Roscommon, and Strokestown.**

1894 Slater's, *Royal Commercial Directory of Ireland*, NLI, lists traders, police, teachers, farmers, and private residents in each of the towns, villages and parishes of the county.

1845- Thom's Almanac and Official Directory. Annual which include references to Roscommon.

In addition, there are also some specialist directories, specifically for medical and religious or ecclesiastical individuals. Some of the National Directories, such as Thom's Directory, will also list a range of professionals (e.g. Lawyers, Military officers etc) from all parts of Ireland. A sample of some of these directories are provided here.

Medical and Religious Directories: Medical directories first appeared in Ireland from the 1840s.
Irish Medical Directory (1872 onwards)
A Complete Catholic Registry, Directory, and Almanack, Vol. 1, 1836
Church of Ireland Directory (1862 to present)
Erck, *Ecclesiastical Register* (1817 and 1830)
Lee, Samuel Percy, *Ecclesiastical Register: Church of Ireland* (1814)
McComb, William, *Presbyterian Almanack* (1857)

Army/Militia: Genealogical Guides in British archives are the PRO Reader's Guides include S. Fowler's *Army Records for Family Historians*, London, 1992, and G. Thomas's, *Records of the Militia from 1757*, London, 1993. See Census Chapter for some lists.

Irishmen who died in the First World War (1914-1918): In 1923 the Irish National War Memorials Commission published memorials of Irishmen who died in the service of the British Army in the Great War of 1914-1918. Copies were provided to major Irish libraries and digitized versions have been published by Eneclann Limited. The 49,400 entries give Name, Regiment Number, Rank, Battalion, Place of Death, and in most cases, Place of Birth.

Attorneys and Barristers: The compilation by E. Keane *et al*, editors, *King's Inns Admission Papers 1607-1867*, Dublin, 1986, is a very helpful source of information on attorneys and barristers in Ireland. In most cases the book lists father's name, address, occupation, mother's maiden name, etc.

Millers: William E. Hogg's *The Millers and Mills of Ireland ... of about 1850*, Dublin, 1997, is a compilation of lists of millers held in the NAI. The original lists can be obtained at the NAI by simply requesting the 'Mill Books'.

Miners: In the 1700s, families like the O'Connors (Mount Allen), the McDermotts (Ballyfarnon), and O'Reillys owned the Arigna iron and coal mines in North Roscommon. In the 1800s, families such as La Touche, Lloyd, and Tenison controlled the industry. Local Arigna families such as Bruen, Flynn, Layden, Leheny, Lynch, Lynn, McTiernan, Noone, and Wynne took control in the twentieth century.[22] The Robert White Papers presented in Chapter 15 (e.g. NLI Ms. 8841) report on the iron and coal works together with rentals relating to lands at Arigna, 1837-1842.

Police: The Irish police force came into being as the Irish Peace Preservation Force in 1814. In 1836 the Irish Constabulary was formed, and was renamed the Royal Irish Constabulary in 1867. During its existence some 90,000 men enrolled. The records are in the PRO in London, and on microfilm in the NAI. They are indexed by initial letter of the surname in two periods i.e. 1816-67 and 1867-1922. The contain the following details: Name; Age when appointed; Height; Native County; Religion; Date of Marriage; Native county of wife; and Dates of appointments, allocations, transfers, promotions; rewards/marks of distinction etc., punishments, etc. It also specifies when discharged, Dismissed, Resigned, Dead or Pensioned. The index and details can be consulted at the NAI (Ref. MFA 24/1-16) or PRO, London (Ref. HO 184.43). RIC Directories for the years 1840-45, 1857, 1876-79, and 1881-1921 are also available at the National Library.[23]

Jim Herlihy's works, which include *The Royal Irish Constabulary: A Short History and Genealogical Guide*, Dublin, 1997, and *The Royal Irish Constabulary: A Complete Alphabetical List of Officers and Men, 1816-1922*, Dublin Four Courts, 1999, provide comprehensive information on researching the 80,000 members of Ireland's pre-1922 police force.

Chapter 12   Newspapers

Newspapers can be a valuable source of family information, although browsing through them can be very time consuming as researchers can be easily distracted by interesting news of the day. Patience, however, may be rewarding.

Newspapers first started in Ireland in the seventeenth century, but there were no newspapers published in Roscommon before 1828. Papers from the surrounding and adjacent counties, including some of those listed on the following pages were in circulation in the county and should be searched. Many of the relevant newspapers are available at the Roscommon County Library (RCL). Also, a number of eighteenth-century Dublin newspapers record notices relating to families in County Roscommon.

Newspapers are particularly useful for the wealthy and professional classes. Before the twentieth century, birth, marriage and death notices were only of the upper classes. However, references to individuals also occur in court cases, advertising and reporting of local affairs.

In addition to the microfilm and hardbound copies available at the NLI, the British Library have excellent microfilm collections. The NLI website, www.nli.ie, in the Online Catalogue, has a useful Newsplan search function where the original and microfilm holdings of Irish newspapers can be found. There is also a subscription website www. irishnewpaperarchives.com. For a subscription fee, the user can pull down images of various Irish newspapers. The following is a listing of County Roscommon newspapers and newspapers of some of the surrounding areas.

Title: Athlone Independent (or Midland Telegraph)
Published: Athlone 11. 1833 - 11.1836
British Library Film and NLI Film

Title: Athlone Sentinel
Published: 11.1834 to 7. 1861
BL Holdings: 21 Nov. 1834 - July 1861
NLI Holdings: 21 Nov. 1834 - 17 May 1854; 18 Apr. - 23 May 1855;
4 July 1855 - 19 Dec. 1859; 8 Jan. 1860 - July 1861.

Title: Boyle Gazette
Published in: Boyle, 1891
NLI Holdings: 1-7.1891
BL Holdings: 2-7: 1891

Title: Galway Express, Mayo, Roscommon, Clare & Limerick Advertiser
Published: 1.1853-9.1920
NLI Holdings: 1885-9.1917 hard copy; 1853-9.1920 mf. (except the above)
BL Holdings: 1.1853-1855, 2.1856-1918, 4.1919-9.1920, hard copy and mf.
BELB Holdings: 1885-9.1920 mf.

Title: Irishman or Galway, Mayo, Roscommon, Sligo & Clare Chronicle
Published: 5-12.1835
NLI Holdings: 5-12.1835 mf.
BL Holdings: 5-12.1835 hard copy and mf.
RCL Holdings: on microfilm, 1819-25

Title: Leitrim Journal and Carrick on Shannon Advertiser
Published: Carrick-on-Shannon, 1850

Title: Roscommon and Leitrim Gazette
Published in: Boyle, 1822-82
NLI Holdings: 1.1841-12.1844
BL Holdings: 4.1822-6.1882

The following are the names of the Sub scribers to this honest
and laudable Socie ty with their respective contributions: --

Captain Ireland	£5 0 0
Thomas Lysaght Esq.	5 0 0
Rev Edward Day	5 0 0
Rev John Madden	5 0 0
John Carsons Esq	5 0 0
Sir Thomas Moriarty	5 0 0
Bernard O'Connor Esq	5 0 0
Joseph Heily Esq	5 0 0
George Brown Esq	2 0 0
John Irwin Esq	2 0 0
John Malone Esq (Dublin)	2 0 0
John O'Farrell Esq	2 0 0
Bartolomew Mahon Esq	2 0 0
Edward Mapother Esq	2 0 0
Edward Corr Esq	2 0 0

*Item on the Roscommon Loan Society from the Roscommon Journal
of the 5th June 1830*

Title: Roscommon Champion
Published from 1935-
NLI Holdings: Original 1935-; Microfilm 1935-1959; 1961-1974;
1975-1985
BL Holdings: Original 19 April 1958, Microfilm, (i) 1986-1992

Title: Roscommon Constitutionalist
Published in: Boyle, 1886-ca. 1891
NLI Holdings: 1.1889-11.1891
BL Holdings: 4.1889-11.1891
RCL Holdings: 1889-91

Title: Roscommon Herald
Published in: Boyle, 1859-current
NLI Holdings: 1.1882-11.1920; 1.1921-in progress
BL Holdings: 4.1859-11.1920; 1921-in progress
RCL Holdings: from 1882

Title: Roscommon Journal and Western Impartial Reporter
Published in: Roscommon, 1828-1927
NLI Holdings: 11.1841-12.1927 (with gaps)
BL Holdings: 7.1828-9.1832; 11.1832-10.1848; 8.1849-12.1918;
3.1919-12.1925
RCL Holdings: 1828-1927

Title: Roscommon Reporter
Published in: Roscommon, 1850-60
BL Holdings: 3.1850-3.1851; 2.1856-3.1859; 10.1860
RCL Holdings: 1850-60 on microfilm

Title: Roscommon Weekly Messenger (continued as Roscommon Messenger in 1861)
Published in: Roscommon, 1848-1935
NLI Holdings: 1.1902-12.1935
BL Holdings: 5.1845-12.1886; 1.1888-12.1935
RCL Holdings: 1848-1935

Title: Strokestown Democrat
RCL Holdings: 1913-48 on microfilm

Title: Telegraph or Connaught Ranger (Castlebar, Co. Mayo)
Published: 1828-1870; 1876-to date (as *Connaught Telegraph*)
NLI Holdings: 9.1830-8.1870 mf.; 6.1879-12.1913. 6.1919-12.1974,
1975 -
BL Holdings: 9.1830-12.1855, 2.1856-11.1856, 2. -8.1870; 5. 1876;
hard copy 1876-1974 MF. Also, 15.12.1869, 12 & 19.1 1870 hard
copy. 9.1830-8.1870 mf.

Title: Tuam Herald (between 1955-1991, known as Herald and Western Adviser)
Published in: Tuam, Co. Galway, 1837-
NLI Film, 1837-1877; 1884-1909; 1911-1923; 1924; 1927-

Title: Western Nationalist (later continued as the Roscommon Champion)
RCL Holdings: on microfilm, 1907-1920
NLI Holdings: 3.1907-4.1920 mf.
BL Holdings: 3.1907-4.1920 hard copy and microfilm.

Chapter 13   Educational Records

Educational records can provide useful information but are often overlooked in genealogical research. They can be productive not only in finding out about students and their families, but also about teachers and administrators.

However State-organised education only started in 1831. Before this, education was provided mainly at a local level by private teachers and 'hedge schools'. In 1733-1734 the Incorporated Society for promoting English Protestant Working Schools in Ireland was granted a charter to start schools to teach scriptures to children of the poor, as well as to educate them in the ways of industry, good husbandry and loyalty to the crown. Over the following century the government funded more than a million pounds for the establishment and running of these schools. Efforts, however, were for the most part unsuccessful in attracting children to these schools.

The major form of education was locally organised 'Hedge Schools' run by private individuals funded by the students. Hedge schools were unlicensed and often in very poor condition and very few hedge school records survive. A history of the period notes "The educational reports for the years prior to 1831 revealed a widespread system of hedge schools in the county. The general picture of these schools was very bad indeed. In some places they were "mud rooms" or "cabins." The school in Derrysra was "a miserable hovel" while the schools in Kilbride were a "wretched hovel" and a "miserable shed," respectively. Schools were held wherever space was available, and many schools were held in chapels."[24] A hedge school in Strokestown was a teacher's house with 63 children. One in Castlecoote was a servant's hall with

107 children; another in Mote Park Demesne was a porter's lodge with 142 children.[25]

The Society for Promoting the Education of the Poor in Ireland, also known as the Kildare Place Society, was founded in 1811. It was the first attempt to introduce systematic, non-denominational primary education. Because of objections by the Roman Catholic hierarchy, the Board of National Education was established in 1831 and it placed control of elementary education with the local clergy in the form of National Schools.[26]

National Schools: The national school system was established in 1831, but it is rare to find a school register of this date. Schools were obliged to keep registers of individual pupils and most registers continue to be stored in the actual schools. Some of these have removed by individuals for safe keeping. Some were lost. Other school registers and roll books are held in the NAI, and are listed in database form on the NAI website. NAI has a card catalogue (extreme right corner of the Reading Room) which provide reference numbers of school records arranged by townland and county. Most of the records pertain to school administration records, but information on teachers and pupils can sometimes be found.

Roscommon County Library holds microfilm copies of Irish Folklore Commission Schools Collection (1937/8) for Roscommon.

University education: Trinity College Dublin was established in 1593 and there was no other university until the 1840s. Trinity students were mainly Church of Ireland, but Roman Catholics also attended. Students from 1637 to 1846 are listed in *Alumni Dublinenses – A Register of the Students, Graduates and Provosts of Trinity College* in the University of Dublin (Burtchaell & Sadlier: London, 1924) also published by Archive CD Books. There are 356 references to Roscommon students.

Before restrictions on Catholic education were finally removed in 1823, an alternative for Catholic young men and some women was to go to continental Europe to study. In particular, Catholic priests were usually educated in this way. Only a very small portion of the Church's archives up to the mid-eighteenth centuries still survives in Ireland today.

FRENCH, FITZSTEPHEN. 1815.

FRENCH, ARTHUR, S.C. (Mr Wigmore, Dungar), Oct. 23, 1708, aged 18 ; s. of John, Armiger ; b. Liverpool. [M.P., Tulsk, 1713–15 ; Co. Roscommon, 1721–27 ; Boyle, 1727–60.]

FRENCH, ARTHUR, Pen. (Mr Grattan), Apr. 16, 1743, aged 16 ; s. of Arthur, Generosus ; b. Dublin. B.A. Vern. 1747. [M.P., Co. Roscommon, 1775–76.]

FRENCH, ARTHUR, S.C. (P.T.), June 3, 1806, aged 18 ; s. of Arthur, Generosus ; b. Co. Roscommon. [1st Baron de Freyne.] See *Foster*.

FRENCH, ARTHUR, S.C. (Dr Burrowes), Oct. 18, 1819, aged 17 ; s. of George, Causidicus ; b. Dublin. B.A. Æst. 1823. M.A. Nov. 1832.

FRENCH, ARTHUR, Pen. (P.T.) Oct. 18, 1830, aged 17 ; s. of Patrick, Generosus ; b. Dublin.

FRENCH, CHARLES, Pen. (Mr Fea), Nov. 6, 1826, aged 29 ; s. of William, de-functus ; b. Dublin.

FRENCH, CHRISTOPHER, S.C. (Dr Norris), Oct. 30, 1771, aged 17 ; s. of Arthur, Generosus ; b. Co. Galway. [Assumed the surname of St George 1774.]

FRENCH, CHRISTOPHER, Pen. (Mr Huddart), Nov. 7, 1825, aged 17 ; s. of Patrick, Generosus ; b. Dublin.

FRENCH, DIGBY. B.A. Vern. 1747. [Incorporated at Oxford 1747–48; s. of Patrick, of Monivae, Co. Galway.] See *Foster*.

FRENCH, DOMINICK, Pen. (Mr Torway, Dublin), Oct. 29, 1684, aged 18 ; s. of

Extract from Alumni Dublinenses: A Register of the Students, Graduates and Provosts of Trinity College 1637-1846

CHAP. IV.]   ECC.   HEREMON GENEALOGIES.   ECC. 435

O'CONOR-ECCLES.

Arms : The Armorial Bearings of " Eccles"* are—Ar. two halberts† crossed saltier-wise az.   *Crest* : A broken halbert az.   *Motto* : Se defendendo.

Sir Hugh O'Conor Dun, of Ballintubbert‡ Castle, county Roscommon, who is No. 124 on the " O'Conor Don" pedigree, was one of the Irish Chiefs who sat in the Irish Parliament of 1585, and signed a Deed of Composition with Queen Elizabeth, as head of his family.   He was Knighted by the Lord Deputy Sir John Perrott, and was styled " Lord of Connaught;" he d. in 1632 at a very advanced age.   Sir Hugh O'Conor Dun m. the daughter of Sir Brian O'Rourke, of Breffni, and by her had several sons.   According to tradition the posterity of the eldest son became extinct since the reign of Charles II.

An extract from O'Hart's Irish Pedigrees (Dublin 1892)

Chapter 14   Gaelic Genealogies

Most family searches in Ireland can not go back further than the beginning of the nineteenth century. However, family researchers remain curious about the origins of their families even if they cannot be traced back further. This chapter is written for those who wish to explore the origins in the older genealogies of families who were situated in the region of what is now County Roscommon.

When delving into the older genealogies, the first step is to go to scholarly sources such as the following to get a general background of the family concerned. These are:

MacLysaght, Edward, *Irish Families, Their Names, Arms & Origins*, Irish Academic Press Limited, Blackrock, Co. Dublin, 1991
------------, *More Irish Families*, Irish Academic Press, Blackrock, Co. Dublin, 1982
------------, *The Surnames of Ireland*, Irish Academic Press, Blackrock, Co. Dublin, 1989
O'Hart, John, *Irish Pedigrees,* Dublin 1892 (see p.106).
Woulfe, Rev. Patrick, *Sloinnte Gaedheal is Gall: Irish Names and Surnames*, Dublin 1923

More detailed searches can then be pursued by Person, Place, Subject or Date in Richard Hayes' *Manuscript Sources for the History of Irish Civilisation* for material catalogued prior to 1965. Hayes's *Manuscript Sources for the History of Irish Civilisation*, First Supplement, 1965-1975, covers material catalogued between 1965 and 1975. Hayes's *Manuscript Sources* can be found in repositories such as the NLI, the NAI, and at the UCD Library. Material catalogued between 1976 and 1990 can be found in the Card Catalogue in the Manuscripts Reading Room of the NLI. Material catalogued from 1990 onwards can be found on the Online Public Access Catalogue (www.nli.ie) of the NLI. In some cases the OPAC refers to Manuscripts Collections Lists which are available in the Manuscripts Reading Room of the NLI.

The NAI website (www.nationalarchives.ie) is also useful as is the CD-ROM *Counties in Time* which was published by the NAI in conjunction with Eneclann Ltd. County and local libraries are also a crucially important resource in locating manuscript sources of genealogical relevance.

Like many other western counties, Roscommon does not have a rich store of records. For example, the Roscommon volumes of the *Civil Survey 1654* have not survived. Neither have the Hearth Money Rolls of the 1660s. The data for Elphin diocese (the largest diocese of County Roscommon) collected in the national religious censuses order by the House of Lords in 1764 and 1766 have also been virtually totally lost.[27]

In spite of these deficiencies, several valuable Roscommon manuscript sources of genealogical relevance are still accessible. These include *Stafford's Inquisition*, the *Books of Survey and Distribution*, the *Transplantation to Connacht 1654 – 58*, Pender's 1659 *Census of Ireland, Books of Survey and Distribution, 1636-1703*, and also the *Census of Elphin 1749*. These are all described in detail in Chapter 5,Census and Census Substitutes.

Two important Roscommon manuscript sources have not as yet become fully accessible to the general public. These are the Coolavin (The McDermot, Prince of Coolavin) and Clonalis (O'Conor Don) archives. In the NLI there is a microfilm (p. 7079) which is a copy of

Ó Duḃḟionn ' (black-ḟionn) ; a rare surname ; found chiefly in Antrim, Cork and Waterford.

Ó Duiḃġeaḋáin—I—Dugidan, Degidan, (Dixon) ; ' des. of Duḃġeaḋán ' ; a Clare surname.

Ó Duiḃġeannáin—I—*O Duigenain*, Duigenan, Duignan, Dignan, Deignan, Duignam, Dignam, &c. ; ' des. of Duḃġeannán ' (dim. of Duḃceann, black-head) ; the name of a distinguished literary family in Co. Roscommon, who were hereditary chroniclers to the Clann Mulrony and Conmaicne, that is, to the MacDermotts, O'Farrells, Magrannells, &c. Their chief residence was at Kilronan.

Ó Duiḃġinn—I—*O Duygin, O Digin*, Digin, Diggin, Deegin, Digan, Deighan, Deegan, Duigan, (Dugan, Duggan, Duggen) ; ' des. of Duḃceann ' (Black-head).

An extract from Irish Names and Surnames
by Rev. Patrick Woulfe (Dublin 1923)

The MacDermot of Coolavin Papers. This is a collection of documents relating to the family of MacDermot and to lands mainly in Co. Roscommon, including a genealogy compiled in 1739. There are 51 items in this collection, c. 1595-1790.[28]

Pedigrees of Irish chiefs who lived in what is now County Roscommon have been recorded in great works such as the *Annals of the Kingdom of Ireland* by the Four Masters which was finished in 1636; *Leabhar Mór Na nGenealach* or *The Great Book of Irish Genealogies* compiled by Dubhaltach Mac Fhirbhisigh between 1656 to 1666; Roger O Ferrall's unpublished Linea Antiqua, 1709, with additions by Sir William Betham (extracts of these three genealogies listed in Appendix 3); and an early, partial pedigree of the O Hara and O Gara chiefs from *Leabhar Uí Eadhra* or *The Book of O'Hara,* the main portion of this manuscript having been written in 1597.

The Royal Irish Academy also holds pedigrees in Irish of Chiefs such as Ferghal O Gara transcribed in the Low Countries between 1655 and 1659. Séamus Pender, Editor, compiled 'The Clery Book of Genealogies', *Analecta Hibernica*, 18, 1951, pp. 1-198. Finally, M.S.O'Brien's, *Corpus Genealogiarum Hiberniae*, (1962) which lists pedigrees and genealogical material from the earliest period down to c. 1500 A.D (in Gaelic).

Another interesting book covering some Roscommon Gaelic genealogies is:

Old Ireland, Tribes and Customs of Hy-Fiachrach, The Genealogies, Tribes and customs of Hy-Fiachrach, commonly called O'Dowd's Country, with a translation and notes by John O'Donovan, Dublin, The Irish Archaeological Society, 1846, Irish Genealogical Foundation, Kansas City, 1993. This book is in both English and Gaelic.

To corroborate and to pinpoint dates of the genealogies of the Roscommon Irish Chiefs, there are three printed primary sources. These works are *The Annals of Connacht (AD 1224-1544)*, *The Annals of Loch Cé*, and the *Annals of the Kingdom of Ireland by the Four Masters from the Earliest Period to the Year 1616*. One can also access these sources online at the CELT Project, University College Cork at http://www.ucc.ie/celt/published.html.

IRISH PEDIGREES;

OR,

THE ORIGIN AND STEM

OF

THE IRISH NATION.

BY

JOHN O'HART,

ASSOCIATE IN ARTS, QUEEN'S UNIVERSITY IN IRELAND ; FELLOW OF THE ROYAL
HISTORICAL AND ARCHÆOLOGICAL ASSOCIATION OF IRELAND ; MEMBER
OF THE HARLEIAN SOCIETY, LONDON ; AUTHOR OF "IRISH
LANDED GENTRY WHEN CROMWELL CAME TO
IRELAND," ETC.

" Where are the heroes of the ages past ?
Where the brave chieftains, where the mighty ones
Who flourished in the infancy of days ?
All to the grave gone down."
—HENRY KIRKE WHITE.

" Man is but the sum of his Ancestors."
—EMERSON.

*Entered according to Act of Congress, in the year 1887, by Richard Oulahan, of
Washington, D.C., in the Office of the Librarian of Congress, at Washington.*

FIFTH EDITION.

IN TWO VOLUMES.

VOL. II.

DUBLIN:

JAMES   DUFFY   AND   CO.,   LIMITED,
15   WELLINGTON   QUAY.

LONDON : BURNS & OATES (LTD.), 28 ORCHARD STREET, W.

GLASGOW : HUGH MARGEY, 14 GREAT CLYDE STREET.

NEW YORK : BENZIGER BROTHERS, 36 & 38 BARCLAY STREET.

1892.

Chapter 15   Surnames and Family Histories

Sir Robert E. Matheson reported the following as the most common surnames in County Roscommon in 1890 based on the names of children born in the year:[29]

Kelly	68	Quinn	25
McDermott	45	Murray	24
Beirne	38	Brennan	22
Regan	35	Higgins	22
Flanagan	32	Towey	22
Connor	30	Kenny	21
McDonagh	26	Flynn	20

According to MacLysaght's individual descriptions in *The Surnames of Ireland*, all of these above listed names are native Irish families which reflect that the Norman invasion had less effect on what is now County Roscommon than on other Irish counties.[30] The following genealogies, family histories and other miscellaneous papers relating to Roscommon families in various archives:

Ailmer: See O'Farrell

Aldworth: See Kelly

Bagot: GO Ms. 178, pp.445-54: Pedigree of Bagot … Carranure, Co. Roscommon & of Melbourne, Australia, c.1575-1862. GO Ms. 109, p.141. Copy of confirmation of arms to descendants of Thomas Neville Bagot of … by Ellen Fallon of Runnimead, Co. Roscommon & to Christopher Nevill Bagot of Aughrane Castle, Co. Galway, in cancellation of arms granted in 1771 of said Thomas Neville Bagot, son of Capt. John Lloyd Bagot & Catherine Cuff of Ballymoe, March 15, 1867.

Balfe: Ainsworth (J.F.): Report on Stapleton Papers (from 1731), in custody of Mssrs. E. & G. Stapleton, solicitors, Dublin, re Dobbyn, Dease, & Balfe families & to lands in Cos. Waterford,, Leix & Roscommon, NLI report on Private Collections, No. 115. Worcester: Record Office: Mss. 705: 24/1799-1801: Indentures etc. re marriage settlement on C.M. Berington & Ellen Balfe re lands of Glans alias Glens alias Glanballythomas, Co. Roscommon, 1858. n.2452 p.1532.

Worcester: Record Office: Mss. 705: 24/1795-8: Copies of wills of James Balfe of Runnemede, Co. Roscommon, dated Jan. 9, 1837 probate Jan. 30, 1841 & of Patrick Balfe, of 29 Marlboro St., Dublin, Dec. 10, 1849. NLI n.2452 p.1532.

Worcester: Record Office: Ms. 705:24/1802: Indenture between Jane Balfe of Runnemede, Katherine Balfe, Ellen Berington & R. Irwin of Emla, Co. Roscommon, trustees of will of James Balfe, re lands of Clonriffe & Knockagonnell, Co. Galway & Glanballythomas, Co. Roscommon, Jan. 3, 1862. NLI n.2452 p.1532.

Worcester: Record Office: Ms. 705:24/1804: Letters, accounts, receipts & other papers concerning estates in Co. Limerick & Co. Roscommon, of Balfe family, 1854-67. NLI n.2452 p.1532.

Worcester: Record Office: Ms. 705:24/1805-6: Rentals & other papers re lands in Glanballythomas, Co. Roscommon, 1854-65. Letters re Glans & Runnimede estates, with incidental papers, 1859-61. NLI n.2452 p.1532.

GO Ms 111d, fol.55-6: Copy of confirmation of arms to descendants of Walter Balfe of Heathfield & to his son, James Balfe of Runnymede, both in Co. Roscommon & to his descendant, Charles Arthur Ulric Felix Chichester, Aug. 10, 1931.

Barnewall: See O'Farrell

Berington: See Balfe

Bingham: See Ormsby.

Blackburn: GO Ms. 139, pp. 243-6: Abstracts of wills of Blackburn of Currihina, Co. Roscommon … & of London, England, 1710-1756.

Bond: GO Ms. 114, pp. 192-5 & 200-3: Pedigree of Bond of Glenlough & Ballyclogher in Co. Derry, of Newton Bond & Lecarrow, Co. Roscommon & of … Co. Longford, 1650-1875.

Boswell (see Tottenham).

Boyce. GO Ms. 111, pp. 107-8: Copy of grant of arms to Robert Henry Boyce, Principal Surveyor of Office of Works, only son of Dr. Robert Boyce of Newtown Barry, Co. Wexford & Myshall, Co. Carlow, second son of William Toura Boyce, elder son of James Boyce of Knockroe, Co. Roscommon, Oct. 19, 1901.

Boyle: NLI Ms. 6147: Lismore Papers: Register of leases made by Richard Boyle, 2nd Earl of Cork, in respect of fishery rights on Blackwater River, & of lands & tenements in counties of Cork, Waterford, Dublin, Wicklow & Roscommon, 1690-1697.

Brabazon: Ainsworth (J.F.): Report on Brabazon Papers (from 1730), re Brabazon family & lands in Co. Roscommon & property in Athlone. NLI Report on Private Collections, No. 18.

Brett: Queries & some information on P. Brett, C. Conroy, Luke Fitzgerald, of Rahara, Co. Roscommon, ...(*Irish Genealogist*, Vol; 3, no. 5, July, 1960).

Bruen: GO Ms. 139, pp. 168-9: Detailed abstracts of wills of Bruen of City of Dublin, of Boyle & of Oak Park, Co. Carlow, 1694-1795

Burke: (See also Fennell). NAI M. 3701: Judges rental of estate of M.A. Burke in Athlone Barony Co. Roscommon, 1898.

GO Ms. 111c, fol. 19: Copy of grant of arms to Sir John Burke, Knt. Of Ravensdale, Strandtown, Belfast, son of Martin Burke, son of Thomas Burke of Highbog, Co. Roscommon, Feb. 11, 1922.

PRONI, T/1750; 1800-c. 1959, 4 pedigrees of ….. Burke family, Roscommon, 1850-1959

Butler/ le Botiller: NLI D. 332: Grant by Philip de Rupella to Sirobald le Botiller of Omany (Hy Many) & Clonodach (Clann Uadach, Cam & Dysart parishes, Co. Rosc.), Sroun (or Croun-Cremhthann, Barony of Killian, Co. Galway) Sukyn (Creagh par.) & Lusmach (Garrycastle Barony, Offaly), Bre (Bray, Co. Wicklow) & le Brun (Co. Dublin), between 1282 & 1285.

NLI D. 331: Grant by Philip de Rupella to Sirobald le Botiller of cantred of Omany & Clonodach in Tyrmany & Croun (parish of Tisrara, Co. Roscommon), etc. (Between 1282 & 1285).

NLI D. 535: Grant by Thomas de ffyhyde (Fifide) to Edmund le Botiller of lands in Trostan, Avenebeg, etc. inodum of Clonodath in Omany (Hy-Many), April 11, 1309.

NLI D. 2803: Exemplification, dated June 9, 1571, of a grant by Phillip de Rupella Toobald le Botiller of lands of Clonenodayne (Clonodach, Co. Roscommon) & other castles, manors, etc. in cantred of Omany, in counties of Galway & Roscommon, March 16, 1283.

GO Ms. 103, P. 118: Copy of grant of arms to Humphry Butler, only son of Hon. John Butler by Margaret, daughter & heiress of John Drury of Kingsland, Co. Roscommon, Jan. 28, 1790.

Byrne: NAI M. 3706: Papers re sale of properties of H.G. Byrne at Ardlagheenbeg & Ballymakerly, Co. Roscommon, 19th c.

Dublin: King's Inns Library: House of Lords Appeals: Vol. 10: Byrne (Gerald) appellant versus Elizabeth Morley executrix of Henry Morley, & James Morley, Jeffery Luther & Michael Waldron executors of George Morley re lands of Ballymacrilly, Rakenelly, & Clonigrossan in Co. Roscommon. Irish Exchequer appeal. a.c. & r.c. Mar., 1730.

Caldwell: Queries & information on …H. Caldwell, wife of E. Wynne, of Toberpatrick, Co. Roscommon… (*Irish Genealogist,* Vol. 1, no. 10, Oct. 1941).

Capel: Hertford: Hertfordshire Record Office: Deeds re estates in Ireland of family of Capel, Earls of Essex, 15th-20th c.

London: British Museum: Harleian Charter 45 D.7: Grant from John de Arderne to Richard de Capella, for his homage & service, of land in tuath called "Crohan" in cantred of Tirmany, Connaught, (c.1360). n.1965 p.1492.

Carson: G.O. Ms. 111c., fol. 103: Copy of confirmation of arms to descendants of John Smyth of Deer Park, Co. Leitrim, & his wife, Frances Lloyd Carson, daughter of John Carson of Annesville, Co. Roscommon & grandson, William Henry Munro Smyth of Hillsborough, Co. Down, son of Thomas Smyth of Abbeyleix, Queen's Co., Jan 19, 1928.

Caulfield (see also Goff): G.O. Ms. 179, p. 318: Pedigree of Caulfield, Lords Charlemont, & of Donamon, Co. Roscommon, c. 1580-c. 1700.

G.O. Ms. 139, p. 56: Detailed abstracts of wills of Caulfield of Donamon, Co. Galway, 1775-1810.

NLI D. 8768: Lease from John Lord Kingston to Thomas Caulfield of quarter of Carbally, Emlaghbeg, etc. in Ballymoe Barony, Co. Roscommon & …. Galway, May, 1, 1668.

Chichester: See Balfe

Collins: GO Ms. 110, pp. 126-7: Copy of confirmation of arms to descendants of William Collins of Lissayegan, Co. Roscommon, & to his grandson, John Tenison Collins of Society Street, Ballinasloe, Co. Galway, eldest son of John Collins of Lower Dominick St., Dublin, Jan. 23, 1891.

Compton: GO Ms. 171, pp.502-4: Pedigree of Compton of Ballyfinegan & Willsgrove, Co. Roscommon & of Castleacres, Glynn, Co. Limerick, c.1710-1838.

Conolly: Ainsworth (J.F.): Report on Conolly Papers (from 1604… re Ballyshannon fishery, Folliott & Conolly families & to lands in Cos. Roscommon. NLI Report on Private Collections, No. 314.

Conroy: G.O. Ms. 178, pp. 290-302: Pedigree of Conroy, formerly O'Mulconry, of Tullon, Co. Roscommon, of Vigoyne, France, of Elphin & Bettifield, Co. Roscommon, Barts., 379 A.D.-1855.

G.O. Ms. 169; p. 333: Pedigree of Conroy earlier O'Mulconry of Fulton, Co. Roscommon, & Conry of Bettyville, Co. Roscommon, of City of Dublin, c. 1570-1825.

Cormick: Ainsworth (J.F.): Report on Cormick Papers (from 1723),

..., re Cormick family & to lands in Cos. Mayo, Roscommon & Westmeath. NLI Report on Private Collections, No. 126).

Cregg: NAI, M 5249 (12): Copies of census returns re family of Cregg, of Co. Roscommon, 1851.

Crofton (see also Dillon): NLI Ms. 8828: Crofton Papers: Correspondence, .. deeds & leases etc re estates of Lords Crofton in cos Sligo & Roscommon, inc letters re extension of railways from Athlone to Sligo, Ballina & Westport, together with Crofton family accounts & a genealogy, c. 1693-1867.

GO Ms. 113, p. 285-95: Copy of Patent of Baronetcy of Crofton of Mote, Co. Roscommon, 1661.

GO Ms. 170, pp. 117-8: Pedigree of Crofton of Mote, Co. Roscommon, Barts. C. 1700-c. 1745.

GO Ms. 182, pp. 395-402 & 429-440: Pedigree of Crofton of Ballymurry, Cambo Castle, Mote, Lisdorne, Toomona, Clonsilla & Castle Ruby, all in Roscommon .... 1540-1937.

D. 10,911-11,054: 144 deeds re property .... of Crofton family of Mote, 1684 to late 19th c.

Ainsworth (J.F.): Report on Crofton Papers (from 1653) ....now in NLI, re Crofton family & to families of McDonogh, Plunkett, St. George, Talbot & Lloyd all of Roscommon & to lands in Roscommon & Sligo. NLI Report on Private Collections, No. 315.

NLI Mss. 4066-4072: Seven diaries of Lady Georgiana Crofton of Mote, 1835-1875.

NLI D. 20,003-7: Two copies of will of Sir Marcus L. Crofton, 1767, will of Sir Oliver Crofton, 1768, will of Sir Edward Crofton, 1736. Deed of Sir M.L. Crofton, 1767, (Croftons of Mote, Co. Roscommon).

NLI Ms. 20, 801: Crofton Papers: Draft deeds & papers re family settlements ... concerning lands in Co. Leitrim, Longford, & Roscommon, 5 items, 1759.

NLI D. 18,562: Lease by Rev. Richard Baldwin .... to Marcus Mowther Crofton of Mote, Co. Roscommon of lands in Dunshaughlin & Grange End, Co. Meath, July 9, 1748.

Crosbie: See Talbot

Cruice: GO Ms. 176, p. 365: Pedigree of Cruice of Carrowneganny, Co. Galway, & Sunnerhill, Co. Roscommon, c. 1720-1850.

Cusack: Ainsworth (J.F.); Report on Cusack family (from 1584), formerly property of Major R. Cusack, Abbeville House, Malahide, now in NLI, re Cusack family & to lands in Co. Dublin & Roscommon. (NLI Rep. on Private Collections, No. 3).

NLI Ms. 8813: Cusack Papers: Documents re transfer of lands at Feltrim, Co. Dublin, by S.J. Bever & J.G. Shields to J.W. Cusack, with documents re purchase of lands at Ballymurray, Co. Roscommon ..., 1832-1857. Also genealogical notes on Cusack family, 1708-1725.

D'Alton: NLI Ms. 20,949: D'Alton papers: Letters to John D'Alton from his mother, Ellen with some references to Co. Roscommon & Westmeath, 3 items, 1806, 1812-13.

NLI Ms. 20,945 D'Alton Papers: Letters from John D'Alton to his wife Kate, mainly decribing his visits to Cos. Roscommon & Westmeath, & also to London, 9 items, 1821-38.

Davies/Davys: GO Ms. 111a, p. 42: Copy of confirmation of arms to descendants of Thomas Davies of Rossleven, Co. Clare & Moate, Co. Galway, eldest son of Walter Davies of Lahinch, Co. Clare & Moate, second son of Thomas Davies of Newcastle, Co. Galway, of Davies family of Cloonshanvoyle, Co. Roscommon & to grandson of Thomas Davies of Rossleven being Seymour George Pilkington Davies of Victoria, second son of Thomas Pilkington Davies of Rossleven, Victoria, Australia, Sept. 17, 1910.

GO Ms. 653: Records of family of Davys of Cloonbonny & Martinstown, co. Roscommon, 1693-1832. (Cuttings of articles from *Longford Leader*).

Devanny: GO Ms. 809, p.11: Report on surname Devanny of Roscommon & adjacent, 1707-1930.

Devenish: GO Ms.111c, fol. 17: Copy of confirmation of arms to descendants of Robert Devenish of Rush Hill, Co. Roscommon, & to his grandson, Robert James Devenish, son of George Devenish, with mention of grant of arms made by Nicholas Narbon, Dec. 4, 1583 to Edmund Devenish of City of Dublin, Feb. 1, 1922.

Dillon: Ainsworth (J.F.); Report on Dillon Papers (from 1405), property of Hon. Ethel Dillon, Clonbrock, Ahascragh, Co. Galway, re Dillon, Greene, McKeogh & Donnellan families & to lands in Cos. Galway & Roscommon. (NLI Rep. on Private Collections, No. 4)

Oxford: Co. Record Office: Mss. Dil. XXII b. 1-2: Dillon Papers. Photograph, made in 1899, of letters patent of Edward III, granting custody of manor of Kilkenny West to Henry Dyllon for 12 years, with translation, 1343. Translation of Confirmation by James I. of manors, castles, towns & lands in Westmeath, Roscommon & Mayo to Sir T. Dillon, 1610. n. 5208 p. 5312.

Oxford: Co. Record Office: Mss. Dil. XXII d. 1-2: Dillon Papers. Notes & letters of Harold Dillon on Dillon family ... Pedigree of family of Dillon of Bracloon Castle, Co. Roscommon, c. 1900. n.5208 p.5312

GO Ms. 172, pp. 52-4: Pedigree of Dillon of Dillon's Grove, Co. Roscommon, … 1180-1800.

GO Ms. 172, pp.52-91: Pedigree of Dillon of Feemore, of Dunboyne, of Proudstown, Co. Meath, of Riverstown, Balgeeth, Lisdornan, Hunstown, Ladyrath, all in Co. Meath, of Twomore, Co. Roscommon of Rath & of Malaga in Spain, c.1180-1953.

GO Ms. 180, pp.480-3: Pedigree of Dillon of Tollaghane, West Rathmile, Springlaun, Co. Roscommon, & Lissiane & Farmhill, Co. Mayo, c.1650-1901.

GO Ms. 182a, pp. 67-8: Pedigree of Dillon of Mount Dillon, & ..Australia, c. 1700-1951.

Dillon (Gerald): Cnoc Diolun (Mount Dillon), a genealogical survey of Dillon family in Ireland. (*Irish Genealogist*, Vol. 2, no. 12, July, 1955).

NLI Ms. 19,676: Clonbrock papers: Album of family photographs [collected by Caroline Dillon (aft. Dealtry)]

NLI Ms. 19,965: Clonbrock papers: Album of newscuttings & misc. papers (collected by Augusta Lady Clonbrock), mainly concerning families Dillon & Crofton

NLI Roscommon Estates Ms. 22,025. Clonbrock family Dillon Papers 1522-1820.

Dodwell: Gray (Edward S.): Three genealogical extracts … of manuscripts, on Dodwells of Manor Dodwell, Co. Roscommon, …. (*Irish Genealogist*, Vol. I, no. 10, Oct., 1941).

Donellan: See Dillon & O'Donnellan

Dowling: See Lynch

Drury: PRONI, T.590: "Photostat" copies of pedigrees of Drury families of Dublin & Roscommon, 1659-1928, compiled by Dr. H.C. Drury.

Queries & some information on Lt. E. Drury, of Kingsland, Co. Roscommon, …. (Irish Genealogist, Vol. I, no. 12, Oct., 1942).

Duckworth: GO Ms. 111, pp. 230-1: Copy of confirmation of arms to descendants of Capt. John Duckworth of Mount Erris, Co. Roscommon, son of Capt. John Duckworth of Mount Erris, & to great grandson of Capt. John Duckworth being Henry Launcelot D'Olier Duckworth, only son of Richard Duckworth, L.R.C.S.I., Aughaslawn in Co. Leitrim, Oct. 15, 1908.

Dundas: NLI Special List 223 Estate Papers Roscommon & Sligo, Dundas Family.

Dunne: GO Ms. 111, pp. 199-200: Copy of confirmation of arms to

Gen. Sir John Hart Dunne, son of John Dunne of Cartrons Lodge, Drumsna, Co. Roscommon, July 20, 1907.

de Exeter: Ms. D. 1501 (7): Inspeximus of an Inquisition taken at Roscommon concerning lands of Richard de Exeter in Connaught, 1301.

Fallon (see also Bagot, French, Kelly): NLI. Ms. 9903: An account of Fallon & Kelly families of Co. Roscommon, entitled "What my grandmother told me", by Maryresa Kelly, Typescript copy, 20th c.

NLI D. 27,080: Copy of marriage settlement of Bernard Fallon of Woodberry, Co. Galway & Mary French of Frenchlawn, Co. Roscommon, 25 Feb., 1829.

GO Ms. 164, p. 213: Pedigree of O'Fallon of Cloonaugh, Co. Roscommon, c. 1690-c.1780.

NLI D. 26,533. Stacpoole Kenny Papers: Marriage settlement of John Fallon of Cloonagh, Co. Roscommon & Helena Maria Rice, of Ennis, Co. Clare, 27 April, 1791, with copy.

Fitzsimons: See O'Connor

Flanagan: See O'Loghlen, Woulfe

Folliot: See King

Foster: GO Ms. 93, pp. 84-7: Pedigree of Foster & Blake Foster of …..Co. Galway & Dromshare, Co. Roscommon, c.1650-c.1850.

Fox: See Lane

French (see also Fallon): GO Ms. 168, p. 246: Pedigree of French of Galway, of Dungar (French Park) & Ennfield & High Lake & Abbey Boyle all in Roscommon, c. 1550-C. 1820.

GO Ms. 169, pp. 431-40: Pedigree of French of Galway, of Dungar (French Park) & Ennfield & High Lake & Abbey Boyle all in Roscommon, c.1550-c.1820.

GO Ms. 171, pp. 395-406: Pedigree of French of Galway City of Gortrassy & of French Park (als. Dungar), of City of Dublin, of Sunfield, Highlake & Oak Park, in Co. Roscommon, 1526-c. 1830.

GO Ms. 173, pp. 24-5: Pedigree of French of French Park incomplete, 1733-c.1800.

GO Ms. 178, pp.496-7: Pedigree of French of Frenchpark, Co. Roscommon, c.1700-c.1800.

NLI D. 27,080: Copy of marriage settlement of Bernard Fallon of Woodberry, Co. Galway & Mary French of Frenchlawn, Co. Roscommon, 25 Feb., 1829.

Ainsworth (Sir John F.) Bart.: Report on papers of family of French, Lords De Freyne, now in NLI, including correspondence, estate &

legal papers, mainly re Co. Roscommon, 17ᵗʰ-20ᵗʰ c. NLI Reports on Private Collections, No. 505.

De Freyne Papers: Correspondence, etc re family of French, Barons De Freyne, mainly re estates in Co. Roscommon, 17ᵗʰ-19ᵗʰ c., (unsorted). See NLI Report on Private Collections, No. 505).

GO Ms. 111E, fol. 9-10: Copy of grant of arms to John French of Mornington Park, Co. Dublin, born about 1808, of French Park, Co. Roscommon, July 3, 1934.

NLI D. 9850: Lease from Right Hon. Diana Countess Dowager of Mountrath to Eyre French of part of lands of Beagh in barony of Athlone, Co. Roscommon, April 30, 1754.

GO Ms. 111B, fol. 64: Copy of grant of supporters to Field Marshall Rt. Hon. John Denton Pinkstone French on his advancement to dignity of Viscount French of Ypres & High Lake in Co. Roscommon, Dec. 21, 1918.

Fry: GO Ms. 111B, fol. 18: Copy of confirmation of arms of descendants of Major Oliver Fry, Royal Artillery, third son of Henry Fry of Frybrook, Co. Roscommon, & to grandson of said Major Fry, being Sir William Fry of Wilton House, Merrion Road, Dublin, third son of William Fry of Dublin, Solicitor, March 3, 1916.

Gately: Papers of Gately family; RCL

Gaynor: PRONI T.2792: Letter from Pat Gaynor, Clooner Blakeny, Co. Roscommon, to General Raines, London re estate matters, 1893. (Photocopy).

Gearty: M. 5249 (28): Copies of census returns re Gearty family of Co. Roscommon, 1851

Gethin: Ainsworth (J.F.): Report on Gethin Papers (from 1678), …, now in NLI, re Ludlow, Dodwell, Plunkett, & Gethin families & to lands in Cos. Meath, Dublin, Westmeath, Sligo & Roscommon. NLI Report on Private Collections, No. 298.

Glass: NLI D. 18,728: Memorial of Chancery bill (filed by Aldborough Writeson at request of John Glass) re lands at Bogginfin, near Athlone, Co. Roscommon, Nov. 25, 1769.

NLI D. 18,735-6: Two copies of a memorial of deed poll from Samuel Windis to John Glass, re filing a bill of discovery of lands of Carrongier & other lands in barony of Athlone, Co. Roscommon, May 21, 1770.

Goff: GO Ms. 108, pp.348-9: Confirmation of arms to descendants of Rev. Thomas Goff & Anne Caulfield & to his son, Thomas William Goff of Oakport, Co. Roscommon, Jan. 7, 1861.

Gore: Ainsworth (J.F.): Report on Palmer Papers (from 1670),…re

Palmer & Gore families & to lands in Cos. Mayo & Roscommon. NLI Report on Private Collections, No. 176.

Grace: GO Ms. 171, pp. 57-8: Pedigree of Grace …. of Mantua, Co. Roscommon, 1534-1818.

Graham: Muncaster Mss.: Papers re planting of Roscommon to be arranged by Sir Ralph Sidley of certain Grahams & others who were giving trouble on Scottish border, 1606. (Hist. Mss. Comm. Tep. 10, App. 4, 1885. pp.258-9, 267).

Grehan: GO Ms. 179, p. 101: Arms of Grehan of Mount Plunkett, Co. Roscommon, 1863.

GO Ms. 109, pp. 13-4: Copy of confirmation of arms to descendant of Patrick Grehan, merchant of Dublin & to his grandson, Patrick Grehan of Mount Plunkett & St. John's, Co. Roscommon, son of Patrick Grehan of Dublin, June 5, 1863.

Greene: See Dillon

Harman: See King

Hatch: NLI Ms. 11339 c. 1775; Seven documents re accounts of Lady Roscommon (deceased).

Hawkes: GO Ms. 802, p. 10: Draft pedigree & copies of deeds of family of Hawkes at Briarfield & Skekyn, Co. Roscommon, 1627–1780.

Heppenstall: GO Ms. 139, pp.2-5: Detailed abstracts of wills of Heppenstall of Kilcroney, Co. Wicklow, of Athleague, Co. Roscommon …., 1796-1805.

Hodson: GO Ms. 141, pp. 18-22: Pedigree & detailed abstracts of wills of Hodson of Hadrew in Buckinghamshire & …. Hodson's bay otherwise Burnes in Co. Roscommon. 1688-1759.

GO Ms. 142, pp. 43-5: Abstracts of deeds of Hodson of Fuerty, Co. Roscommon, of Athlone, Co, Westmeath & Coolkenna, Co. Wicklow, 1709-1714.

RIA: Upton Papers, No. 21: Pedigree & notes on families of Hodson of Hodson's Bay, Co. Roscommon, … 20th c.

RIA: Upton Papers, No. 9: Copies of wills of W. Hodson, St. John's, Co. Rosc. Jan. 1794: J. Hodson, Bp. Of Elphin, July 1685; ….

Houston: GO Ms. 141, pp. 73-6: Detailed abstracts of wills of Houston of … Ashgrove, Co. Roscommon, 1676-1888.

Hughes: NLI D. 16,836-7: Deeds between Henry Hughes of Beechwood, C. Roscommon, & Owen Wynne of Hazelwood, Co. Sligo, concerning lands of Corbo, Co. Roscommon, Aug. 23, 1783, & concerning lands in Ballintobber, Co. Roscommon, May 7, 1789.

Hussey: GO Ms. 111, pp.228-9: Copy of grant of quarterings of Valentine John Hussey Walsh of Mul Hussey, Co. Roscommon &

Canby, France, son of Walter Hussey Walsh of Cranagh & Mul Hussey by Ellen, daughter of Valentine O'Brien O'Connor of Rockfield, Co. Dublin, being son of John Walsh, son of Patrick Hussey Walsh by Margaret, only daughter & heir of John Hussey by Jane, daughter & heir of John Moore, Oct. 2, 1908.

Hynde: GO Ms. 141, p.143: Detailed abstract of will of George Hynde of Castlemeaghan, Co. Roscommon, 1711.

Hyde: NLI Ms. 17,998: Four letters re proposal to present to Douglas Hyde full title to his property occupied by him at Ratra, Co. Roscommon, 1908.

Ireland: GO Ms. 177, pp. 313-9: Pedigree of Ireland; Lords of Hutte & Hale in Co. Lancashire, & of de Courcey Ireland of Irelande Grove, of Low Park, Co. Roscommon…. c. 1066-1875.

Irwin: (see also Balfe, Ormsby) G.O. Ms. 141, pp. 299-307: Detailed abstracts of wills of Irwin of Leybeg & Oran in Co. Roscommon, of Londonderry, …, 1709-c. 1850.

GO Ms.111a, p.41: Copy of confirmation of arms to descendants of Col. Richard Irwin, eldest son of Richard Irwin, son of Richard Irwin all of Rathmoyle, son of Arthur Irwin of Fernhall, son of John Irwin of Ballinderry all in Roscommon & to eldest son of said Col. Irwin, being Arthur John Irwin of Rathmoyle, 1910.

GO Ms. 172, p. 155: Pedigree of Irwin of Rathmoyle, Co. Roscommon, 1580-1927.

GO Ms. 806, p.7: Notes on history of "Irwin of Rathmoyle" with draft pedigrees, draft confirmations, etc., 1580-1912.

Gray (Edward Stewart): Irwins of Roxborough, Co. Roscommon & Streamstown, co. Sligo. (*Irish Genealogist*, Vol. I, no.2, Oct., 1937).

Jebb: GO Ms. 141, p. 200: Detailed abstracts of wills of Jebb of Drogheda & Boyle, 1767-1771.

Johnston: NAI M. 6195: Letters dismissory on departure of Rev. Gideon Johnston from Diocese of Achrony where he held vicarages of Castlemore, Co. Roscommon, Killmoves, Co. Mayo, & Killcolman, Co. Roscommon, Aug. 15, 1705.

Jones; NAI D. 17,367-9!: M. 2075-§: Deeds & other papers re estate of Ballyfinny, Co. Roscommon, & in Dublin & Co. Meath of Jones family, 1682-1707.

Kelly/ O'Kelly (see also Fallon): NAI M. 2748: Copy of a petition by Brian Kelly, & order on same, for a patent for lands in Cos. Roscommon & Galway, n.d. (between 1592 & 1610).

M 5249 (34): Copies of census returns re Kelly family of Co. Roscommon, 1851.

NLI n. 5297 p. 5406 O'Kelly Papers: Family letters in possession of Count John D. O'Kelly of Gurtray, Portumna, Co. Galway concerning family of O'Kelly de Gallagh & Tycooly, Co. Galway, & family of Plunkett of Mount Plunkett & Keelogues, Co. Roscommon, 1772-1828. (For details, see Special List No. 78).

NLI Ms. 8157: "Photostat" copy of some notes (by R.A. Butler of Skerries) on families of Kelly in Counties Galway & Roscommon, c. 1921.

GO Ms. 164, pp.66-7: Pedigree of O'Kelly of Gallagh, Co. Galway & Tycooly, Co. Roscommon, Counts of Holy Roman Empire, c.1650-1782.

GO Ms. 164, pp. 204-10: Pedigree of O'Kelly of Aughrim, Co. Galway & Keenagh, Co. Roscommon, c.1350-c.1750.

GO Ms. 165, p. 400: Pedigree of O'Kelly of Gort & Killahan, Co. Roscommon, c.1600-c.1750.

GO Ms. 175, pp. 12-24: Pedigree of O'Kelly & Kelly with descent from Art Mac Con, father of Cormac Mac Art, Princes of Imaine, Chiefs of name, of Gallach & Mullaghmore, of Aghrim, of Cloher, of Athleague, & of Cargins & Castle Ruby in Co. Roscommon…, A.D. 195-1841.

GO Ms. 177, pp. 240-1: Pedigree of O'Kelly (called de Galway), Lords of Imaine, of Clogher, of Aghrim & of Low Countries, c. 1200-c.1850.

NLI. Ms. 9903: An account of Fallon & Kelly families of Co. Roscommon, entitled "What my grandmother told me", by Mary Teresa Kelly, Typescript copy, 20th c.

G.O. Ms. 180, pp. 571-5: Pedigree of family of Kelly of Ballyforan & Kilcash, Co. Roscommon, & Muckloon, Co. Galway, of Weston, Co. Meath, c. 1600-c. 1907.

GO Ms. 162, pp. 98-100: Pedigree of Denis O'Farrell (born O'Kelly) of Cambo, Co. Roscommon, of Clonlyon, Co. Galway, of Aghrane, Co. Galway & Sckryne, Co. Roscommon, c.1325-1755.

GO Ms. 143, pp.111-2: Detailed abstracts of wills of Sankey of Newpark, Co. Longford, with reference to Kelly of Kellybrook, Co. Roscommon, 1767-1859.

NLI Ms. 19,723: Volume of extracts from Irish history, mainly with reference to O'Connor & Kelly families, collected by John Kelly, of Essex Lawn, 1856.

NLI D. 26,724-26,728: Exemplification of recovery concerning members of Kelly family re lands in Cos. Galway & Roscommon, 5 items, 1701-1804.

GO Ms. 809, p. 14, Miscellaneous pedigrees of Kelly of Skreen, Co. Roscommon, 1674-1832, Kelly of Dublin, 1837-1934, & Bryan Kelly, husband of Margaret, daughter of Sir William Aldworth, c. 1670.

GO Ms. 182, pp.265-70: Pedigree of Kelly & O'Kelly, Lords of Iath Maine, of Aughrim, of Keenagh, of Buckfield, all in Co. Galway, of Strokestown, Co. Roscommon, & of City of London, & City of Dublin, c. 1700-1904.

Kenney: GO Ms. 108, pp. 245-§: Certificate of arms to Lt. Jacques Louis Lionel Kenney, Knight of Legion of Honour & of St. Stanislaus of Russia, only son of Thomas Henry Kenney of Ballyforan, Co. Roscommon & Derrymore, Kings Co., younger brother of Lt. Col. James Fitz Gerald of Kilclogher, Co. Galway with details of French descent & ancient ancestry, Oct. 22, 1858.

GO Ms. 178, pp. 250-5: Pedigree of Kenney of Kenney in Somerset, …& Ballyforan, Co. Roscommon & of France, 1165-1858.

King / Kingston (see also Caulfiedl, Stafford, Harman): NLI, Ms. 8472: King Papers: Letters & other documents re King family of Charlestown & Elphin, Co. Roscommon, especially to John King, M.P., 1667-1787.

The Kings of King House: Story of the Descendants of Sir John King of Boyle & their Estates at Michelstown, Rockingham & Newcastle. A.L. King-Harman, Bedford, 1996

NLI Ms. 2177: Estate & household accounts of John King of Roscommon, 1707-1736.

NLI Ms. 11,346: Agreement between Hon. Henry King & Charles Nesbitt concerning letting of Kileglass, May 16, 1789.

NLI Ms. 8810; 1673-1838, Documents re King family, Rockingham, Co. Roscommon & Mitchelstown, Co. Cork, 1673-1838. inc accounts of Countess of Rosse.

GO Ms. 169, p.131: Pedigree of King of Rockingham, Co. Roscommon c.1700-1824.

PRONI, D/4168, 1770-1872; papers of King-Harman family of King House & Rockingham, Boyle, Co. Roscommon & Michelstown Castle, Co. Cork, comprise 440 documents & 15 volumes.

G.O. Ms. 87, p. 89: Funeral certificate of Catherine, Lady (John) King, mother of Sir Robert King of Abbey Boyle who married Hon. Frances Folliot & of John King, Clerk of Hanaper who married Margaret, daughter of Francis Edgeworth Dec. 14, 1617.

Portland Mss. Petition of Sir R. King to House of Commons stating his services & losses, including taking of his house at Boyle about Aug.

1, 1646 by Marquess of Clanricarde, Oct. 1, 1646. (Hist. Mss. Comm. Rep. 13, App. 1, 1891. p. 394).

GO Ms. 113, pp. 283-4: Pedigree of King, Barts., of Charlestown, Co. Roscommon, c.1580-1815.

GO Ms. 106, p. 79: Copy of grant of arms to descendants of Rt. Rev. Edward King, Bishop of Elphin & to Gilbert King of Charlestown, Co. Roscommon ...Dec. 12, 1814.

NLI Ms. 8472: King Papers: Letters & other documents re King family of Charlestown & Elphin, Co. Roscommon, especially to John King, M.P., 1667-1787.

Ainsworth (J.F.): Report on King Papers from 1604, property of Sir C. Stafford King-Harman, re King family & to lands in Cos. Roscommon..... NLI Report on Private Collections, No. 105.

NAI Co. 1975: Exemplification of record of action on writ of covenant before Common Bench, 1684, by Standish Hartstrong, of Dublin, & Robert Choppyne of Newcastle v. Robert Lord Kingston for lands in Cos. Sligo & Roscommon.

GO Ms. 110, pp.39-40: Copy of grant of arms to Henry Ernest Newcoman King, Earl of Kingston & to his wife, Florence Margaret Christina, Countess of Kingston, only surviving daughter of Edward King Tenison of Kilronan Castle, Co. Roscommon, on assuming Royal Licence name & arms of King Tenison, March 29, 1883.

Kirkwood: GO Ms. 108, pp.235-6: Confirmation of arms to descendants of James Kirkwood of Woodbrook in Co. Roscommon & his grandson, James Kirkwood of Woodbrook, July 19, 1858.

Knott: Reynolds (H.F.): Testamentary records of …. R. Knott of Knockadoe, Co. Roscommon, 1784. (Irish Genealogist, Vol. I, no. 12, Oct., 1942).

Lambert: Marsh's Library, Dublin: Ms. 23. 2. 6: (Extracts). Commissions of scire facias, concerning certain debts, issued against R. Lambert of Castlestrange, Co. Roscommon, heir of P. Hill of Castlechichester, Co. Antrim & T. O Monk of Newtowne St. Albans, Co. Louth, 1632-3.

Lane/Lane-Fox: (See also Muschamp) Ainsworth (J.F.): Report on Lane-Fox Papers (from 1661), ...now in Central Library, Leeds, re Fox & Lane families, & to lands in Cos. …. Roscommon. NLI Rept on Private Collections, No. 414.

Egmont Mss.: Grant to Sir Richard Lane of Tulsk, Co. Roscommon & to Sir J. Perceval of all fairs & markets in Ireland forfeited by reason of rebellion & not already granted. 1662 (Hist. Mss. Comm. Rep. Egmont Mss. Vol. II., 1909, pp.4/5.

Grant of Arms to Richard Lane of Tulsk," *Irish Roots*, Issue No. 50, 2004, p. 11.

MacLysaght (E.A.): Lane Papers .. now in NLI. *Analecta Hibernica*, No. 15, 1944.

Lawder: G.O. Ms. 182, pp.96-113: Pedigree of Lawder of Drumsna, Ashford, Tully, Kilmore, Aughamore, Longfield & Kilclara in Co. Roscommon, of .... Co. Leitrim, Kansas, America, & of Malay States, c. 1520-1908.

L'Estrange: GO Ms. 177, p.136: Pedigree of L'Estrange of Moyston in King's Co., of Castle L'Estrange in Roscommon, through Moore & Toke from Chichele, c. 1400-c.1700.

Lion: NLI 16 I. 14 (2) Manuscript map: Survey of Abby Cartron, Co. Roscommon, in possession of Edmd. Lion of Elphin... & several others. By Fiagh Kelly. June 1717.

Lloyd (see also Crofton): G.O. Ms. 168, pp. 246-9: Pedigree of Lloyd of Croghan, of Fairview of Lisdurn, of Rockville, all in Co. Roscommon, c. 1680-1813.

GO Ms.812(12): Draft pedigree of Lloyd of Rockville, Co. Roscommon, 1748-1916.

Papers of Lloyd family of Crohan, 1660-1935; RCL

Lynch: see More-O'Ferral

Lyster (see also West.): GO Ms. 111, pp.59-60: Copy of confirmation of arms to descendants of Thomas Lyster of Grange & to his great great grandson, Col. Frederic Torrens Lyster of Warren House, Starcoross, Co. Devon, son of Major Thomas St. George Lyster of Grange, Co. Roscommon, Dec. 21, 1899.

GO Ms. 111, pp. 60-1: Copy of confirmation of crest to descendants of Anthony Lyster of New Park, Co. Roscommon & to his great grandson, John Sanderson Lyster..., Queensland Defence Forces, eldest son of Lt. Col. George Fosbery Lyster, Dec. 21, 1899.

Lynch: NLI D. 11,291: Copy of a Conveyance from Very Rev. Jonathan Swift, Dean of St. Patrick's, Edmond Dowling, & others, to Alexander Lynch, .. lands of Kiltee, Rapheak... in barony of Moycarnon, Co. Roscommon, July 29, 1732.

MacCormack: GO Ms. 818 (11): Draft pedigree of MacCormack of Baslick, Co. Roscommon, c. 1850-1933.

MacDermott: G.O. Ms. 165, pp.249-53: Pedigree of MacDermott, of Leimgarr in Co. Roscommon, c. 1270-1774

G.O. Ms. 87, pp. 183-6: Pedigree of Macdermott of Leimgarr, Co. Roscommon & of Island of Jamaica made for Michael McDermott, Aid Major in Sheldons Regiment, c. 354-1765

G.O. Ms. 169, pp.393-404 & 413: Pedigree of McDermott, Lords of Moylurg, of Carrig & Leigarr & Kilronan & Camagh & of Castle McDermott all in Roscommon & of Fadden & Toomevara in Co. Tipperary, 956-1824.

NAI. M. 5651 (1-2): Papers re property of Owne McDermott, a minor, in Springfield, Ballymoe, Barony Co. Galway & in Co. Roscommon (subsequent owner Mrs. Eliza O'Loughlin).

NLI P. 7079, MacDermot of Coolavin Papers: Collection of documents re family of MacDermot & to lands mainly in Co. Roscommon, including genealogy compiled, 1739; 51 items, c. 1595-1790 (Originals in possession of MacDermot, Coolavin, Ballaghaderreen, Co. Roscommon, 1795)

NLI Ms. 8719: 'Photostat' copies of a genealogy of Mulrony Mac Dermott, Lord of family of Mac Dermott, of Moylurg, Co. Roscommon, "who emigrated to France", compiled from Annals & other chronicles, & attested by John O'Harte, Bishop of Achrony, 1739.

GO Ms. 179, pp. 329-34: Pedigree of MacDermott Roe of Camagh also Alderford, Co. Roscommon, 1744-1865

McDonogh: see Crofton

McGan: NAI M. 6166: Lease of Arthur Lord De Freyne to James McGan of a plot in Sheepwalk, Tibohine parish, Co. Roscommon, Oct. 10, 1851.

McKeogh: See Dillon

MacManaway: GO Ms. 111B, fol. 47: Copy of grant of arms to … Terence MacManaway of Tarmon.. & his grandson, Ven. James MacManaway, Archdeacon of Clogher, son of John MacManaway of Coolougher, Roscommon, Dec. 10, 1917.

GO Ms. 819(23): Draft pedigree & draft confirmation of arms of MacManaway of Coolougher, Co. Roscommon, c.1800-1917.

Magennis: See Plunkett

Mahon: NAI. M. 5752: Papers of case of Payne v. Conry, c. 1830, containing information on Mahon family of Co. Roscommon, with a statement of title of Maurice Mahon Ramsay to Crohane & Ballykerin, Co. Tipperary, citing documents 1755-1857.

NLI D. 15,442: Lease by R. French to N. Mahon of lands in Aghaclogher, Barony & Co. of Roscommon, March 3, 1731 (1732).

GO. Ms. 180 Pedigree of Mahon of Ballinemly & Strokestown, of Cavetown all in Co. Roscommon, Barons Hartland, C. 1650-c. 1830

GO. Ms. 139, p. 150, abstract of will of Nicholas Mahon of Ballinenly.. 1677

GO Ms. 107, pp, 362-363: Copy of grant of arms being Mahon quartering Pakenham to Henry Sanford Pakenham, son of Very Rev. Henry Pakenham, D.D. Dean of St. Patrick & to his issue by daughter & heir apparent of Denis Mahon of Strokestown, Co. Roscommon on his assuming under Royal License & in compliance with desire of said Denis Mahon, name & arms of Pakenham Mahon, April 15, 1847. GO Ms. 110, pp. 51-2: Copy of confirmation of arms to descendants of Robert Mahon of Cavetown, Co. Roscommon & to his grandson, Lt. Col. Maurice Hartland Mahon, son of Rev. Arthur Mahon of Cavetown, Feb. 2, 1884.

Mapother: GO Ms. 813 (15): Draft pedigree & information as to Mapother of Kiltivan, Co. Roscommon, 1625-1802.

Mason : NLI D. 8767: Lease from Sir John Parker to Robert Mason of lands in Clonnyn, Barony of Devlin, Co. Westmeath, Lugboy, Tullyquarter & other lands in Barony of Ballintubber, Co. Roscommon, Feb. 18, 1695.

Montgomery: NAI French Pres. 1928: Certificate of a decree by Commissioners to … Hugh Montgomery & Capt. Hugh Montgomery concerning premises in Dublin & lands in Co. Roscommon & Leitrim, March 22, 1666 (1667).

Morley: See Byrne

Morton: NLI Ms. 13n715: Ten letters to Susan Morton, Castlenode, Strokestown, 1835-1849, mainly on business affairs from (K.C.?) Packenham.

Mulhall: Queries & some information on ….Mulhall family of Boyle. (Irish Genealogist, Vol. 2, no. 10, July, 1953).

Muschamp: NLI. Ms. 10990, 1696-1706, Misc. legal documents in Irish Chancery suits between William Spencer, Ballinasloe, Co. Roscommon & Denny Muschamp & wife, Lady Lanesborough

More O'Farrell: NLI Ainsworth (J.F.); Report on More O'Farrell papers (from 1543)… re O'More or More, O'Reilly & O'Ferrall families & to lands in Cos. Mayo, Dublin, Roscommon, Meath & Kildare. Report on Private Collections, No. 253.

King's Inns Library Dublin: House of Lords Appeals: Vol. 4a: Moore (Garrett) appellant versus John Henry Lynch & others re estate of John Moore of Brees, Co. Mayo who died in 1635, including lands of ….. Clonbigney & Carrowreagh in Roscommon. …. includes Moore family pedigree; Mar, 1744.

GO Ms. 164, p. 67: Pedigree of O'Moore of Cloonbigny, Co. Roscommon & Annaghbeg, Co. Galway, c.1650-c.1750.

Mulloy: GO Ms. 169, pp. 417-420: Family of Mulloy of Oughteriry & Hughestown & Oak Port, all in Co. Roscommon, c. 1580-1856.

GO Ms. 171, pp. 351-5: Pedigree of Mulloy (formerly O'Mulloy), chiefs of name, of Oughterhiry & Lacken, Co. Roscommon, of Kilmanaghan & Aghadenagh in Kings Co. & Oakpark, Co. Roscommon, 405 A.D.-1824.

GO Ms. 178, pp. 153-8: Pedigree of Mulloy of Oughterheera & Hughestown, & of Oakport all in Co. Roscommon, c.1580-1856.

GO Ms. 182, p.p. 56-8: Pedigree of Mulloy, later O'Mulloy, of Hughestown, Co. Roscommon, c.1800-1909.

GO Ms. 820 (16): Draft pedigree of Gorges Mulloy of Hughestown, c. 1750-1909.

Naughten/ Naghten: (see also O'Naghten) G.O. Ms 182 a, pp. 86-86: Pedigree of Naughten of Clonark, Athlone, & Thomastown Park, Co. Westmeath, of Woodpark House, Co. Roscommon & Innis Lonnaught, Co. Tipperary, c. 1775-1953

NLI D. 8766: Lease from Richard, Earl of Ranelagh to Laughlin Naughten of quarter of Clonarke (Co. Roscommon), Feb. 3, 1680.

GO Ms. 111H, fol. 13: Copy of confirmation of arms to descendants of Thomas Naughten of Drum, Co. Roscommon & to his grandson Martin Naughten, M.D., of Innis-lonaught, Clonmel, Co. Tipperary, son of Patrick Naughten of Woodbrook, Co. Roscommon, Oct 5., 1953.

Newcoman: see King

Nugent: GO Ms. 174, p.55: Pedigree of Nugent of Gillstown, c.1600-c.1690.

Oakes: NAI M. 3231: Letters of presentation of Rev. George Oakes to parish of Bumlin, Elphin Diocese, July, 1835.

O'Casey/ O'Caiside: British Museum: Ms. Egerton 178: …. autobiography of & poems by Tomás O'Caiside… 1782. NLI n.234 p.408

O'Connell: Ainsworth (J.F.): Second supplementary report on O'Connell Fitzsimon Papers (from 1687), property of Lt. Col. M. O'Connell Fitzsimon, Glencullen House, Co. Dublin, re O'Connell & Fitzsimon families & to lands in Co. Roscommon & Meath & Dublin City. NLI Report on Private Collections, No. 361.

O'Connor (see also Hussey, Kelly): NLI Ms. 25,271 Ballintuber (Co. Roscommon). Pedigree of O'Connor of Castleruby, Tuomona & Ballintuber, Co. Roscommon, & of Dublin, etc., showing descent from O'Connor, Kings of Connaught 1156-1898

G.O. Ms. 169, pp. 254-61, Pedigree of O'Connor, Kings of Connaught

& Monarchs of Ireland & O'Conor Don, of Ballintobber & of Clonalis & of Bealnager in Co. Roscommon, 364-1824

G.O. Ms. 182, pp. 583-4; Pedigree of O'Conor Don of Belangare & Clonalis, Co. Roscommon, & Lucan House, Lucan, Co. Dublin, & Lake Park, Roundwood, Co. Wicklow, c. 1800-1946

G.O. Ms. 180; pp. 346-8 & 357: Pedigree of O'Conor Don, of Belangare & Mount Druid & of Palace Elphin all in Co. Roscommon, 1732-1880

GO Ms. 111d, fol. 85-6: Copy of confirmation of arms to descendants of Roderick O'Conor of Milton in Co. Roscommon & to his great grandson, Aylward Robert O'Conor of Somerton Lodge, Dun Laoghaire, elder son of Aylward Owen Blood O'Conor of Dublin, July 4, 1932.

Fr. Casey Ms.: Domestic & farm accts. & personal memoranda, kept largely in Irish by Charles O'Conor, Belnagare, 1742-1745. NLI n. 3317 p. 2935.

GO Ms. 110, pp. 124-5: Confirmation of arms to descendants of Thomas O'Conor of Newgarden & to his grandson, Nicholas Roderick O'Conor, C.B., C.M.G., H.M. Minister in Bulgaria, eldest son of Patrick O'Conor, both of Dundermott, Sept. 4, 1890.

NLI Ms. 19,723: Volume of extracts from Irish history, mainly with reference to O'Connor & Kelly families, collected by John Kelly, of Essex Lawn, 1856.

O'Donell: Salisbury Mss.: Submission of Shane Mac Manis oge O'Donell, of Tyrconemm, for himself & others, at Abbey of Boyle, Feb. 19, 1598. (Hist. Mss. Comm. Salisbury Mss. Pt. VIII., 1899, p. 56).

GO Ms. 169, pp.1-32: Pedigree of O'Donnell, Monarchs of Ireland, Lords of Tirconnell, … of Greyfield, Co. Roscommon; … B.C.1370-A.D.1812.

GO Ms. 112, pp.238-44: Pedigree of O'Donnell, Prince of Tyrconnell, Barons Donegal & Earls of Tirconnell, … of Greyfield in Co. Roscommon, ….., c.1400-1811.

GO Ms. 179, pp.369-71: Pedigree of O'Donel of Greyfield, c.1760-1865.

Manchester: John Rylands Library: Ms. 498, inc. O'Dugan's genealogy of O'Donnellans, 1750.

O'Farrell: (See also Kelly, More) Salisbury Mss.: Petition to Lord Burghley of Iriell O'Farrell for manor & rents of Grannard, as 3 abbeys of Clowntwoskerte, Kilmore & Iherirke have been taken up by Sir P. Barnewall & Nicholas Ailmer (between 1586 & 1598). (Hist. Mss. Comm. Rep. Salisbury Mss. Pt. XIV., 1923, p. 71).

GO Ms. 111a, p.15: Copy of confirmation of arms to descendants of Harward O'Farrell of Minard, Co. Longford, & to his great grandson, Sir George Plunkett O'Farrell, third son of Harward O'Farrell, M.D., of Tangier House, Co. Roscommon, son of John O'Farrell, Aug. 11, 1909.

O'Hara: (see also Trench) NLI Ms. 20,304, O'Hara Papers, c. 1765-1842, letters to Charles O'Hara from members of Trench family, including his cousin, Charlotte Trench, Ashford, Co. Roscommon, c. 1765-1842

GO Ms. 3, pp. 106-7: Letter of Charles O'Hara of Nymphsfield from Boyle, July 14, 1794

NLI Mss. 14,328-32: O'Loghlen papers: 5 small note-books (of Mrs. John Woulfe Flanagan, née Susan O'Loghlen?) giving domestic expenses at Drumdoe, Boyle, Co. Roscommon, 1851, 1854, 1855, 1863, 1865).

O'Kelly: See Kelly

O'Loghlen: NLI Ms. 14,334: O'Loghlen Papers: Accounts of Capt. John W. Flanagan, in account with National Bank, Boyle, Co. Roscommon, 1867-1869.

O Maolalla/ Mullally: Manchester: John Rylands Library: Ms. 498, including genealogy of O Maolalla. Inscription on Athlone bridge, erected 1567.

O'Mulconry: See Conroy.

O'Mulloy: See Mulloy

O'Naghten: (see also Naughten). NLI Ms. 21,928 Pedigree, genealogical notes O'Naghten, Co. Roscommon & Cuba 1956-57.

GO Ms. 95, p. 75: Pedigree of O'Naghten of Athlone & Thomastown with descent from O'Kelly of Killahan all in Co. Roscommon & of Gort, c.1660-1788.

GO Ms. 165, pp.400-3: Pedigree of O'Naghten of Thomastown, Co. Roscommon, Co. Roscommon, c.1600-1788.

O'Reilly: (See also Moore). NLI D. 18,632: Assignment of mortgage by Thomas Macklin of Dublin to Edward Geoghegan, of Kill, Co. Galway, & John Tracy O'Reilly, of Dublin, of lands in Kill, Moat & other lands in Co. Galway & Clonerigh, Co. Roscommon, Nov. 20, 1802.

Orwark: Salisbury Mss.: Submission of Bryan Orwark to Queen at Abbey of Boyle, Feb. 18, 1598. (Hist. Mss. Comm. Salisbury Mss. Pt. VIII. 1899, p. 55).

O'Rourke: Salisbury Mss.: Treasons found by inquest against Brian O'Rourke. He procured A. McConnell & Donell McConell to rebel

& also one Tadg O'Harte who burned Ballimote. O'Rourke burned Ballinglass in Roscommon & killed O'Kenan & C. Cadwell. He burned Knockmullin in Barony of Tirerrell, Co. Sligo & killed Cheneam Wood (1591). (Hist. Mss. Comm. Salisbury Mss. Pt. IV., 1892, pp. 170-71).
Ormsby: G.O. Ms. 182, pp.92-4: Pedigree of Ormsby of Louth, Co. Lincoln, of Lisagallon & Ballymurray, Co. Roscommon.
Belfast, PRONI: D. 896 (Cont'd): Deeds to lands in Kilmore, Co. Roscommon of Ormsby & Bingham families, 1738-1892. ....
Gray (Edward S.): Some notes on two Irish families. Irwins of Fermanagh & Donegal, Ormsbys of Tobervaddy, Co. Roscommon (*Irish Genealogist*, Vol. I, no.9, April, 1941).
Packenham: see Mahon, Walsh
Palmer: See Gore
Peyton: GO Ms. 174, pp. 128-53: Family of Peyton ...Suffolk, ... of Boyle, Roscommon, of ... Co. Leitrim, and of Cartrona, Co. Roscommon, c. 1100-c. 1840.
Gray (Edward S.): Four Irish pedigrees.... Peyton, of Corregard House, Co. Roscommon .. , (*Irish Genealogist*, Vol. 2, no. 2, Oct., 1944)
Plunkett (see also Crofton, Kelly): GO Ms. 165, pp. 240-2: Pedigree of Plunkett of Dunhagly in Co. Dublin, of Markee, Co. Sligo & Kilamod in Co. Roscommon, & ...Poland, c. 1550-1774.
NLI D. 24,461: Probate of will of Patrick Plunket of Elm Park; May 30, 1809.
NLI D. 27,172: Baker Papers: Settlement by Patrick Plunkett of Castleplunkett, Co. Roscommon, on George Talbot & others, in consideration of marriage of his son James Plunkett & Mary, daughter of Arthur Magennis, late Viscount Magennis of Iveagh, concerning lands at Liscloghan, Co. Roscommon, 12 Jun., 1688.
Potts: NLI Ms. 3150: "Photostat" copy of a typescript schedule of title deeds & other documents re properties of Lieut.-Col. J.W. Hastings Potts of Newcourt, Athlone, in counties Westmeath & Roscommon. Documents date from 1700 to 1909.
Radcliffe: GO Ms. 804(12): Report on family of Radcliffe of Castle Coote, Roscommon & Thorold, Ontario, 1689-1844.
Radigan: GO MS. 111H, fol. 94: Copy of grant of arms to descendants of John Radigan of Rathmore, Four Mile House, Co. Roscommon & to his son John Bernard Radigan, Knight Commander of Order of Dr. Gregory, of Gary, Indiana, on application of latter's son, Dr. Leo Robert Radigan, June 26, 1958.
Roscommon: See Hatch Papers above.

St. George: (see also Crofton, Wills) GO Ms. 170, pp. 111-24: Pedigree of St. George of Halieverton in England, … of Hatley St. George, …, (Barts.), c.1100-1817.

Sandford (see also Wills): NLI Ms. 9120: Letters patent creating Henry Moore Sandford Baron Mount Sandford of Castlerea, Co. Roscommon, with a special remainder of title to his two brothers William & George Sandford, 31 July, 1800.

NAI D. 8002-8160: M. 531-544: Deeds & maps re property of Sandford family in Co. Roscommon, from 1723.

GO Ms. 94, pp.64-5: Pedigree of Moore Sandford, Baron Mount Sandford of Castlerea in Co. Roscommon, c.1680-1805.

Sandys: G.O. Ms. 172, p. 215: Pedigree of Sandys of Derham Lodge, 178-1924.

NAI. Collis & Ward; parcel 20, 1743-1898.

Sankey: See Kelly

Simpson: G.O. Ms. 172, p. 215: … Papers re estates of Simpson family in Scurloge, Bush, Levittstown, & Rochestown, Co. Wexford, Leevy, Corlea & Corlasky, Co. Leitrim & in Cos. Leix & Roscommon, 1743-1898.

Slacke: GO Ms. 108, pp. 374-5: Copy of confirmation of arms to descendants of William Slacke of Annadale, Co. Leitrim & to his grandson, Rev. William Randal Slacke of Ashleigh, Co. Down, son of Dr. William Slacke, M.D., of Strokestown, Co. Roscommon, June 21, 1861.

Smith: Trinity College Library, Dublin: Misc. Box IV.: Two page abstract of life of W. Smith, rector of Aughrim, Co. Roscommon, 1765-1835.

Spencer: See Muschamp.

Stafford: GO Ms. 111, pp.65-66 & 207-8: Copy of grant of arms to Edward Charles Stafford of Rockingham, Co. Roscommon, a minor, eldest son of Thomas Joseph Stafford by Frances Agnes King Harman, only daughter of Rt. Hon. Edward Robert King Harman on his assuming under Royal Licence name & arms of Stafford King Harman, Feb. 10, 1900.

GO. Ms. 111, pp. 206-7; Copy of confirmation of arms to descendants of John Stafford, son of Thomas Stafford, both of Portobello, son of Hugh Stafford, son of John Stafford, both of Elphin, youngest son of Thomas Stafford of Gillstown, who died 1733, & to son of first mentioned John, being Thomas Joseph Stafford, Dec. 16, 1907.

GO Ms.111,pp.207-8: Copy of certificate of arms, being Harman quartering King & Stafford, to Edward Charles Stafford King Harman of Rockingham, Dec. 16, 1907.

GO Ms.111d, fol.105-6: Copy of grant of arms being Harman quartering King & Stafford to Capt. Cecil William Francis Stafford of Rockingham, Co. Roscommon, 2nd son of Rt. Hon. Sir Thomas Joseph Stafford, Bart., by Frances Agnes, only daughter of Rt. Hon. Edward Robert King Harman of Rockingham on his assuming name & arms of Stafford King Harman, Sept. 24, 1933.

Stafford (John), of Gillstown, Roscommon, father of Margaret, Mrs.Theophilus Blakeney, information sought. (The Genealogists' Magazine, Vol. 5, no. 3, Sept., 1929).

GO Ms.114, pp.158-9: Pedigree of Stafford, Barts., later Stafford-King-Harman, Barts., of Taney House, Dundrum, Co. Dublin & Rockingham, Co. Roscommon, 1857-1914.

Stanley (see also Wills): GO Ms. 176, pp. 374-82: Pedigree of Stanley of ….. of Low Park, Co. Roscommon, of Gardenrath, Co. Meath, c. 1720-1851.

Staunton: NLI D. 11,290: Copy of a deed between Edmond Dowling, Very Rev. Jonathan Swift, Dean of St. Patrick's, & others; & Thomas Staunton; leading to uses of a fine of lands of Killtee, Rapheak, & other denominations in barony of Moycarnon, Co. Roscommon, May, 1730.

Talbot (see also Crofton): NLI, Ms. 22,825, correspondence of Talbot family, Mount Talbot, Co. Roscommon, early 19th century-1945, mainly family letters.

GO. Ms. 174, p. 1-2: Pedigree of Talbot, Mount Talbot, Co. Roscommon, later Crosbie, c. 1700-1816.

NLI D. 11,429: Marriage agreement between Anthony Carroll of Emmill, King's Co., & Lucy Talbot of Mount Talbot, Co; Roscommon. Jan 19, 1737 (1738).

GO Ms. 152, pp. 128-3& : Copy of royal licence to John Talbot Crosbie of Mount Talbot in Co. Roscommon to take name & bear arms of Talbot, Sept. 23, 1851.

GO. Ms. 107, pp. 408-9: Copy of grant of arms being Talbot quartering Crosbie & Hamilton, to John Crosbie of Mount Talbot, Co. Roscommon, on his assuming … in compliance with will of his late uncle, William Talbot of Mount Talbot, name & arms of Talbot, Nov. 7, 1851.

NLI D. 11,288: Copy of a mortgage from William Taylor & Annabella his wife, Sir Samuel Cooke, Kt., & others to Very Rev. Jonathan Swift, Dean of St. Patrick's, of lands of Killtee, Rapheak, & other denominations in barony of Moycarnon,… June 24, 1721.

Tenison (see also Collins): NLI D. 27,369-27, 377 Deeds re family of Tenison & allied families in Dublin & in Co. Roscommon 1758-19th-20th Century, 9 items.

GO Ms. 169, p. 131: Pedigree of Tenison of Castle Tenison.., c.1760-1824.

Toler: G.O. Ms. 110, pp. 57-8: Copy of grant of arms of Hector James Charles Toler of Beechwood, Co. Roscommon, son of Rev. Peter Toler by Marianne Aylward, eldest daughter of Nicholas Aylward of Shankill Castle, Co. Kilkenny, on his assuming under Royal Licence name & arms of Toler Aylward, Sept. 29, 1884.

Tottenham: Ainsworth (J.F.): Report on Tottenham Papers (from 1663),…now in NLI, re Boswell & Tottenham families in Cos.Roscommon….. NLI Report on Private Collections, No. 182.

Ainsworth (J.F.): Rept on Tottenham Papers (from 1641) …now in NLI, re Boswell & Tottenham families & to lands in Cos. Roscommon …. NLI Report on Private Collections, No. 51.

Ainsworth (J.F.): Supplementary Rept on Tottenham Papers (from 1743)… on microfilm in NLI, re Tottenham, Eccles, & Boswell families & to lands in Cos. Roscommon …NLI Report on Private Collections, No. 386.

Trant: GO Ms. 106, p. 93: Copy of confirmation of arms to descendants of Domenick Trant of Dunkettle, Co. Cork & his grandson, Henry Trant of Rathmile, …. 1816.

Trench: (See also O'Hara) NLI M. 11,368: Domville Papers. About 250 misc. documents, inc. rentals & sketch maps re Trench estates in Queen's Co., Mayo & Roscommon, 19th c.

NAI M. 371: Map of estate of Frederick Trench at Clonagh, Co. Roscommon, 1777.

Walker: Ainsworth (J.F.): Report on Walker papers (from 1726)… re Athlone Corporation, Adamson, Handcock, Kelly, Longworth, Robinson & Rochfort families & to lands in Cos. Roscommon & Westmeath. NLI Report on Private Collections, No. 196.

NAI M.6988: Docs re property … of Walker family in Cos. Meath & Roscommon, 1666-1880.

Walsh/Walshe (see also Hussey): G.O. Ms. 160, pp. 63-4: Pedigree of Walsh of Carrickmaine & Belcarrow, of West Indies, & of Flanders, c. 1525-1721.

G.O. Ms. 171, pp. 491-2: Pedigree of Le Waleys of Carrickmaye, Co. Dublin & Bellecarrow, Co. Roscommon, 1381-1838.

GO Ms. 111a; p. 17: Copy of grant of arms to descendant of Thomas Walsh of St. Helena Lodge, Co. Roscommon, by Mary, eldest daughter and co-heir of Robert Packenham of Athlone & to grandson of said Thomas, being Alfred Redley Packenham Walsh, eldest son of Rt. Rev. William Packenham Walsh … Sept. 3, 1909.

NLI Ms. 14,033-4: Cuttings & notes compiled by R.D. Walshe re Co. Roscommon at large (14,033), & places, etc., in Co. Roscommon in alphabetical order (14,034), c. 1915.

West: GO Ms.111, pp.157-8: Copy of confirmation of arms to descendants of Alderman Mathew West of Ederney, son of Mathew West of Dublin & brother of James West of Fort William, Co. Roscommon & to grandson of said Alderman Mathew West, being Lt. Augustus George West of White Park, son of Rev. William James of Ederney, Co. Fermanagh, Nov. 7, 1904.

GO Ms. 105, p. 30 & p31;   GO Ms. 150, pp. 71-3: Copy of grant of arms to James West of Fort William, Co. Roscommon on assuming … in accordance with will of John Lyster of Dublin, name of Lyster, Dec. 19, 1805.

Weston: Weston Papers: Letters Vol. III. Letter from Lord Kingsborough to Edward Weston on personal affairs, Boyle, June 10, 1748 (Hist. Mss. Comm. Rep. 10, App. 1, 1885. p. 301).

White: NLI Ms. 8845: Robert White Papers: Legal documents re Court proceedings to which Robert White was a party, mainly in respect of Arigna mines, together with criminal proceedings against Thomas Flattery & James Benson for conspiring to murder Robert White, c. 1804-1857.

NLI Ms. 8856-8857: Robert White Papers: Letters to & drafts or copies of letters of Robert White, mainly concerning his business interests, including Arigna & Languin, France, mines, & legal cases in which he was involved, c. 1830-1850.

NLI. Ms. 8841: Robert White papers: Reports on iron & coal works at Arigna, Co. Roscommon, in which Robert White had an interest, together with rentals re lands at Arigna, 1837-1842.

NLI Mss. 8853-8854: Robert White Papers: Letter from John O'Donovan to Robert White re family of Whyte, & letters to him from Messrs. Symes & Keller, Solicitors, in relation to Arigna mines, 1840-1845.

NLI Ms. 8848: Robert White Papers: Copies of letters by Robert White to W.H. Ash-Hurst, lawyer, & to Mr. Stratford, his conducting clerk…, 1842.

NLI Ms. 8858: Robert White papers: Prescription for cure of fever & dysentery, together with "Mr. Boyer's soup receipts for use of poor", with a note by Robert White stating it had been copied for benefit of poor labourers at Arigna mines, 1847.

Wills: NAI, Ms. 999/671, 1774-1839, includes 20 November 1802 settlement of marriage of William Robert Wills, Wills Grove, Co. Roscommon, & Olivia St. George, Kilcolgan, Co. Galway.

NLI Ms. 3203: Miscellaneous notes & abstracts of public & other records by H. S. Guinness on family of Stanley & Wills family of Willsgrove & Castlerea House, Co. Roscommon, 1932.

GO Ms. 152, pp.52-4: Copy of royal licence to William Robert Wills of Willsgrove & Castlerea in Co. Roscommon to take name of Sandford … Sandford, April 12, 1847.

GO Ms. 107, pp.372-3: Copy of grant of arms, being Wills quartering Sandford, to William Robert Wills of Willsgrove & Castlerea in Co. Roscommon on his assuming for himself & his issue by Mary Grey Sandford under Royal Licence name & arms of Wills Sandford, Sept. 13, 1847.

GO Ms. 110, pp. 109-10: Copy of grant of arms to Edward Wills Sandford of Castlerea House, Co. Roscommon, second son of Thomas George Wills Sandford of Castlerea, on his assuming … in compliance with will of his grandfather, William Robert Wills Sandford, name & arms of Wills Sandford, Jan. 28, 1889.

Woulfe: NLI Ms. 14,318-27: O'Loghlen Papers: 10 small diaries or memoranda books of John Woulfe Flanagan, Dromdoe, Boyle, Co. Roscommon, various dates, 1841-1867.

Wynne (see also Hughes): Townshend Mss.: Letter of C. Wynne of Hazelwood, Co. Sligo, to Lord Townshend, … Jan. 1, 1769. (Hist. Mss. Comm. Rep. 11, App.4, 1887. P405).

NLI D. 16,835: Deed between James Wynne of Longford, Co. Sligo, & Roger Dowdal of Tonrege, Co. Sligo, concerning lands in Kilmore, Co. Roscommon, April 25, 1745.

GO Ms. 174, P.149: Pedigree of Wynne of Tobberpatrick, Co. Roscommon, 1695-1806.

Yeadon: GO Ms.168, p.246: Pedigree of Yeadon of Abbey Boyle…, c.1650-c.1750.

Young (See also Ormsby): GO Ms. 108, pp. 205-6: Copy of confirmation of arms to descendants of Owen Young…& to his descendant, James Young, only surviving son of Owen Young & grandson of Capt. Mathew Young all of Harristown, …Jan, 9, 1858.

The above list of surnames is by no means exhaustive and researchers should also consult the records of the GO card index and the online search facility, and also *Hayes'Manuscript Sources*. When researching Irish families a very important reference to utilise is Virginia Wade McAnlis 'Consolidated Index to the Records of the Genealogical Office, Dublin, Ireland - Vol.1-4, Surnames A-Z, 1994-1997' which is available at the NLI and on CD Rom.

(Mac) DOCKERY   This name is seldom found outside its original habitat viz. Co. Roscommon, where before the destruction of the Gaelic order it was the duty of O'Flanagan, O'Beirne and Clan Dail-re-deacair (branches of the Silmurray) to guard the preys or spoils of O'Conor, the last named being specially charged with the provision of straw for encampment and furniture and beds for O'Conor's house. In its original form the sur-name, MacDail-re-Deachair, is of a rare and interesting type. It was first anglicized as MacGallredocker – in 1582 and again in 1591 several men of that name re-ceived pardons with others in Co. Roscommon; in 1585 in a similar official document it appears as MacGilldogher, which is presumably a clerk's attempt to write down Mac Giolla Deacair phonetically, for even as early as that this synonym was coming into use. According to Woulfe the corrupt modern form is Ó Dochraidh, and O'Dockery is now used as the anglicized form when the prefix is not omitted; but there is no doubt that Dockery is properly a Mac not an O name.

Sir Henry Dowcra, the Elizabethan commander in the war against O'Neill, whose name was sometimes spelt Dockewray in contemporary documents, was of course English and had no connexion with the Roscommon sept. This, no doubt, is the same name as Dockerey, which was found in the Pale in the fifteenth century.

Matheson records the use in Meath of Harden as synony-mous with Mac Dacker. Woulfe states that Hardy and Hardiman are also so used. Such cases are very rare.   Map

The entry for the surname (Mac) Dockery in
'Mac Lysaght's - More Irish Surnames'

Chapter 16   Miscellaneous Sources

Emigration: John Grenham's *Tracing Your Irish Ancestors*, Gill & Macmillan, Dublin, 2006, is an excellent reference on Irish emigration.
- Indexes such as *In Search of Missing Friends*, NEHGS, and the Ellis Island records, www.ellisisland.org, also have significant entries of Roscommon emigrants.
-Emigrants From Ireland 1847-1852, State-aided Emigration Schemes from Crown estates in Ireland by Eilish Ellis, Genealogical Publishing Co. Inc. (1993). Includes the estate of Ballykilcline, Kilglass, Co. Roscommon p.10-21

History of Roscommon: NLI Mss. 5141-5145: Typescript copies of material for a history of County Roscommon, by Rev. Michael O'Flanagan.
- NLI Ms. 4608: A bibliography of the writings of Walter A. Jones of Strokestown, mainly on the antiquities, folklore, family and local history of Co. Cork and Co. Roscommon, c.1940.

Public Elections and Politics: NLI Ms. 1550: Miscellaneous extracts on the political, ecclesiastical and social history of the Midland and Western counties of Ireland since the 13th century made by Malachy Moran, 19- . With Indexes.
- NLI Ms. 8933: Harrington Papers: Letters to Timothy C. Harrington relating to the activities of the Irish National League in counties … Roscommon etc, 1880-1888.
- NLI Ms. 10,122: Pakenham-Mahon Papers: Documents on Grand Jury, magistracy and finance matters relating to Co. Roscommon, 1786 and 1809-1858.

- NLI Ms. 10,149: Pakenham-Mahon Papers: Note of a meeting in Roscommon c. 1861 to appoint a committee on local land improvement.

Rebellion Papers: Hastings Mss.: Warrant from Sir A. Chichester for pardons to a number of persons named, mostly from Co. Galway, Co. Roscommon and Co. Sligo, Dublin, July 6, 1609. (Hist. Mss. Comm. Rep. Hastings Mss. Vol.IV., 1947. p. 36).
- Trinity College Library Dublin: Ms. 830 (F. 3. 1): Originals of authentic copies of the examinations…for inquiring into the losses …cruelties…during…the Rebellion in 1641, to…1660.   Counties Roscommon and Galway.
- NAI Q.R.O. Papers: Lists of innocents for Counties Clare, Galway, Meath, Mayo and Roscommon with denominations of lands held by them, 1675.
- Fortescue Mss.: Letter of the Marquis of Buckingham to Lord Grenville on the disturbances in Mayo, Sligo and Roscommon and the campaign against tithes led by Capt. Thrasher, and on the Castlebar trials and the ineffectual action of the government. With copy of Grenville's reply. Dec. 11, 14, 1806. (Hist. Mss. Comm. Rep. Fortescue Mss. Vol. VIII., 1912. pp. 463-8).
- Salisbury Mss.: Letter of H. Cuffe to E. Reynolds concerning the defeat of Sir Conyers Clifford at the Curlieu Hills near Boyle. Dublin, Aug. 11, 1599. (Hist. Mss. Comm. Rep. Salisbury Mss. Pt. IX., 1902. pp. 289-90).

Tours of the County Roscommon: NLI Ms. 5628: Tour through Roscommon County by John Keogh, and a table of the baronies and parishes of Connaught, Mid 19th cent.

The William Smith O'Brien Petition: This petition signed between 1848 and 1849 by 70,000 people in Ireland and 10,000 people in England, helped to commute the death sentence of one of the leaders of the 1848 rising, William Smith O'Brien, from a death sentence to transportation to Australia for life. The original records are at the NAI. *Eneclann also have a CD-ROM called the 1848 Petitions: the William Smith O'Brien Petition*, which may be worthwhile perusing for Roscommon ancestors.

Chapter 17   Further Reading

This chapter lists further general reference works and sources of background reading on the history, culture and people of Roscommon. Printed works such as books, booklets, and journal articles can help provide a better understanding of the historical and cultural background of a locality. The listing in this chapter aims to provide information which will help to identify new sources of information.

Roscommon Local Journals and Books
Journal of the Roscommon Historical and Archaeological Society. NLI Ir 94125 r 5
Index to Co. Roscommon Historical & Archaeological Society Journal Vols. I –V, RCL
Journal of the Old Athlone Society. Journal published on an occasional basis since 1969. Copies available at: NLI Ir 94131 o 1
The Irish Connection (Co. Roscommon Family History Society - annual)
Athlone: Materials from printed sources relating to the history of Athlone and surrounding areas, 1699-1899", NLI Mss 1543 -7.
Beirne, Francis M., A *History of the Parish of Tisrara.* Tisrara Heritage Soc.1997
Beirne, Francis, editor, The *Diocese of Elphin; People, Places and Pilgimage*, The Columba Press, Blackrock, Co. Dublin, 2000,
Burke, Francis *Lough Cé and its annals: North Roscommon and the diocese of Elphin in times of old*, Dublin, 1895. NLI Ir 27412 b 1
Burke, William P. *The Irish Priests in Penal Times (1660 – 1760)*, Irish University Press, Shannon, (1st edition, 1914), reprint 1968
Byrne, Vincent, *A Thousand Years of the Hidden Annals of the Kingdom of Connaught, 366-1385 AD*, Scanway, Dublin, 2000

Clarke, Desmond "Athlone, a bibliographical study", *An Leabhar,* No. 10, 1952, 138-9

Coleman, Anne, *Riotous Roscommon: Social Unrest in the 1840s* Irish Press, Dublin, 1999

Connolly, S.J., *Priests and People of Ireland, 1780 – 1845*, Four Court Press, Dublin, 2001

Corish, Patrick and Sheehy, David, *Records of the Irish Catholic Church*, Irish Academic Press, Dublin, 2001

Counties in Time; Documents and Commentaries from the National Archives of Ireland, Eneclann, Dublin, 2004 CD-ROM

Coyle, Liam, *A Parish History of Kilglass, Ruskey and Slata*, published by Kilglass Gaels, no date, RCL

Cronin, Timothy, History of Roscommon, Volume III, 1612-1670, R 941.75, Roscommon, 1977, unpublished, RCL

Cronin, Timothy, Notes on the History of Roscommon, unpublished, RCL

Cronin, Timothy, The Foundations of Landlordism in the Barony of Athlone 1566-1666, unpublished, RCL

Dalton, E.A., *History of the Archdiocese of Tuam,* Dublin, 1928

Dooley, Terence, *Sources of the History of Landed Estates in Ireland*, Irish Academic Press, Dublin, 2000

Drum & Its Hinterland, Its History, and Its People, First Edition, 1994, Drum Heritage Group, Athlone

Egan, Patrick K. *The parish of Ballinasloe, its history from the earliest times to the present day*, Dublin, 1960.

Fallon, Rosaleen, *A County Roscommon Wedding, 1892*, Four Courts Press, Dublin, 2004

Farrell, Noel, *Exploring Family Origins in Old Roscommon Town*, self-published, Longford, 1998

Feely, Colin. Feelys of Boyle, Draftsmen in Stone for Over Two Hundred Years, unpublished, RCL

Finerty, Mary, "The Roscommon Estates of the Lords Crofton, 1845-95", unpublished, RCL

French, Maurice, *The Frenchs of French Park*, self-published,, Warminster, Wilts, 1999,

Friel, Frank, *Roscommon County Council, 100 years of Local Government, 1899 to 1999.* Herald Printworks, Boyle, undated

Gacquin, William, "1821 Census Fragments for Co. Roscommon," *Roscommon Historical & Archaeological Soc. Journal*, Vol. 7, 1998

Gacquin, William, "Eskerbaun, County Roscommon," *Irish Townlands: Studies in Local History*, Dublin, Four Courts Press, Dublin, 1998

Gacquin, William, *Roscommon Before the Famine, The Parishes of Kiltoom and Cam, 1749 – 1845*, Irish Academic Press, Dublin, 1996

Hayes, Richard, editor, *Manuscript Sources for the History of Irish Civilisation*, Volume 8, Places, L-Z, G.K. Hall & Co., Boston, 1965

Hayes, Richard, editor*, Manuscript Sources for the History of Irish Civilisation*, First Supplement, 1965-1975, Volume 2, Subjects, G.K. Hall & Co., Boston, 1979

Helferty, Seamas & Refausé, Raymond, editors, *Directory of Irish Archives*, Third Edition, Four Courts Press, Dublin, 1999

Howley, Brenda, "The Arigna Mining Experience," *The Corran Herald*, Ballymot Heritage Group, Issue 38, 2005/2006

Hunter, John, *Resource County Roscommon, Ireland*, published by John Hunter, Queensland, Australia, 2004

Index to the Prerogative Wills of Ireland, 1536-1810, & Supplement, Sir Arthur Vicars, Archives CD Books Ireland, Dublin 2005 CD-ROM

Index to Griffith's Valuation of Ireland, 1848 – 1864, Family Tree Maker, Heritage World and the Genealogical Publishing Co., Broderbund, 1998 CD-ROM

Keaney, Marion *Athlone bridging the centuries*, Westmeath county council, Mullingar, 1991. NLI Ir 94131 a 2

Knox, H.T., *Notes on the Early History of the Dioceses of Tuam, Killala, and Achrony,* Hodges, Figgis & Co. Ltd., Dublin, 1904

Lawler, Ruth, ed. *The 1848 Petitions, William Smith O'Brien Petition*, Irish Records Index Vol. 2, Records at the NAI, CD ROM, Eneclann Ltd., Dublin, 2001,

Leahy, David, *County Longford and Its People*, Flyleaf Press, Dublin, 1990

Lenehan, Jim, *Politics and Society in Athlone, 1830-1885, A Rotten Borough*, Irish Academic Press, Dublin, 1999

Lyons, MaryAnn, editor, Dooley, Terence, *Sources for the History of Landed Estates in Ireland*, Irish Academic Press, Dublin, 2000

MacDermot, Dermot, *MacDermot of Moylurg*, MacDermot Clan Association, Manorhamilton, County Leitrim, 1996

MacNamee, James J. *History of the Diocese of Ardagh*, Dublin, 1954.

McAnlis, Virginia Wade, *The Consolidated Index to the Records of the Genealogical Office, Dublin*, Issaguag, Washington, 1994

McDermot, Lady Betty, *O'Ruairc of Brefne*, Dunlavin, Co. Wicklow, 1987

McDonnel-Garvey, Máire, *Mid Connacht: the Ancient Territory of Sliabh Lugha,* Drumlin Publications, Manorhamilton, Co. Leitrim, 1995

McGowan, Eileen, "Surnames of County Roscommon," *Irish Roots*, No. 1, 1993

McGreevy, Dr. John, S.S.C., *Emigrant and Emigré, George Thomas Plunkett, Easpag Aillfine, 1814-1827*, NLI, Dublin, 1992

Manning, Peter, 'Review of *The Census of Elphin 1749*,' *The Irish Genealogist*, Vol. 11, No. 4, Irish Genealogical Research Society, London, 2005

Matheson, Sir Robert E., LL.D., *Special Report on Surnames in Ireland [Together with] Varieties and Synonymes of Surnames and Christian Names in Ireland*, Genealogical Publishing Co., Baltimore, MD, 1994

Mattimoe, Cyril, *North Roscommon: Its People and Past*, 1992

Monahan, Rev. J. *Records Relating to the Diocese of Ardagh and Clonmacnoise*, 1886.

Moran, James M., *Stepping on Stones: Local History of the Ballinturly/Correal Valley in the Suck Lowlands, Roscommon Mid-West,* Athleague, Co. Roscommon, 1993

Moylurg Writers, Boyle, *A Selection of Articles on Places, Buildings and Events of Local Interest*, Roscommon Herald, Boyle, 1988,

Moylurg Writers, Boyle, *A Selection of Articles on Places, Buildings and Events of Local Interest*, Volume 2, Roscommon Herald, Boyle, 1993

Murtagh, H. *Irish Historic Towns Atlas: Athlone,* RIA, Dublin, 1994.

Murtagh, H. *Athlone besieged,* Temple Printing Co., Athlone, 1991. NLI Ir 94107 p 21(1)

O'Brien, Brendan *Athlone Workhouse and the Famine,* Old Athlone Society, Athlone, 1995. NLI Ir 300 p 207(8)

O'Brien, Gearoid, *St. Mary's Parish, Athlone, A History*, St. Mel's Diocesan Trust, Longford, 1989

O'Callaghan, Miceál, *For Ireland and Freedom: Roscommon's Contribution to the Fight for Independence, 1917-1921*, Boyle, Co. Roscommon, 1964

O'Conor, Roderic, *Memoir of a Controversy respecting the Name Burne by The O'Connors of Ballintubber; The Title of Don, and the Legal representatives of the family*, Her Majesty's Stationery Office, Dublin 1857,

O'Connor Don Papers, List of Manuscript Sources, Clonalis, Castlerea, Co. Roscommon, Gilbert Library Ms. 203, RCL

O'Connor, Patrick, *The Royal O'Connors of Connaught*, Old House Press, 1997

O'Donovan Name Books County Roscommon Vol. 114 Elphin to Kilmore

O'Donovan Letters Vols. 1 & 2, Letters Containing Information Relative to the Antiquities of the County Roscommon collected during the progress of the Ordnance Survey in 1837 vol. Bray 1931.

O'Donovan, John, *The Tribes and Customs of Hy-Many, Commonly Called O'Kelly's Country,* Irish Archaeological Society, Dublin, 1843, repub. Irish Genealogical Foundation, Kansas City, 1992

Ryan, James, editor, *Irish Church Records*, 2nd edition, Flyleaf Press, Dublin, 2001

Smith, Brian, *Tracing Your Mayo Ancestors*, Flyleaf Press, Dublin, 1997

Smythe-Wood, Patrick, editor, *Index to Kilmore Diocesan Wills*, Stroud, Glos.,, undated

Stokes, George T. *Athlone, the Shannon & Lough Ree*, Dublin & Athlone, 1897. NLI Ir 91413 s 1

Swords, Liam, *A Dominant Church; The Diocese of Achrony 1818-1960*, The Columba Press, Dublin, 2004

Swords, Liam, *The Hidden Church; The Diocese of Achrony 1689-1818*, The Columba Press, Dublin, 1997

Taughmaconnell a History, compiled by the Taughmaconnell Historical and Heritage Group, Athlone, October 2000, RCL

The Irish Genealogical Foundation, *Genealogy & Family History of County Roscommon*, Irish Genealogical Foundation, Kansas City, MO, 2003

Travers, Charles, *Roscommon, The Untold Story*, 1994, Herald Printers, Boyle, 1994,

Ward, Robert, & Coogan Ward, Catherine, eds., *Letters of Charles O'Connor of Belangare*, Vol.1 (1731-1771), Vol.2,(1772-1790) Irish American Cultural Institute

Ward, Robert, Wrynn, John, and Coogan Ward, Catherine, editors, *Letters of Charles O'Conor of Belangare*, The Catholic University Press, Washington, D.C., 1988

Weld, Isaac, *Statistical Survey of the County of Roscommon*, Royal Dublin Society, Dublin 1832, RCL

Chapter 18   Useful Information

This chapter contains contact information, websites and descriptions of repositories and other organisations which may be useful to the Roscommon researcher.

Roscommon County Library (RCL)
Abbey Street, Roscommon, Ireland.
Telephone (0903)6637277: Fax (0903)6637101
E-mail: roslib@iol.ie or roslib@eircom.net
Website: www.iol.ie:~roslib

There are seven public libraries serving the county. The major local history collection is in the Roscommon town branch, but all have material of relevance. The collection includes: Boards of Guardians Minutes; Minutes of Boyle Dispensary District, Board of Health; County Council, Pension Committee and Roscommon Town Commissioners; and Grand Jury Records. It also houses microfilms of other material of local interest, including Moran Manuscripts 1548-50; Reverend John Keogh's Statistical Account of Co. Roscommon; and Irish Folklore Commission Schools Collection (1937/8). Further information, and opening times can be obtained from the website www.iol.ie:~roslib

Roscommon Heritage and Genealogy Company (RHGC)
Church Street, Strokestown, Co. Roscommon.
Telephone: (078) 33380; Fax: (078) 33398
Email: **info@roscommonroots.com**
Website: **www.irishroots.net/Roscmmn.htm**;
          www.roscommonroots.com

This is the designated Irish Family History Foundation (IFHF) centre serving Co. Roscommon and offers a fee-based genealogical research service. The IFHF is the coordinating body for a network of government-approved genealogical research centresthat have computerized tens of millions of Irish ancestral records of different types. RHGC has access to over a million genealogical records including:

o   Church Records pre 1900
o   Civil Records pre 1900
o   Tithe Applotment Land Records circa. 1820
o   Griffith's Valuation Land Records circa. 1850
o   1901 Census
o   1749 Elphin Diocesan Census
o   Trade Directories
o   RIC Indices
o   Freeholder's Lists
o   Current Voters Lists

It also holds other historical materials pertaining to individual parishes

Local History & related Societies

Aughrim and Kilmore History Group
Mrs. Kathleen O'Dowd, Kilcroy, Hillstreet, via Carrick-on-Shannon, Co. Roscommon

Ballaghaderreen Museum and Art Centre, Ms. Bernadette Jordan, Cortoon, Ballaghaderreen, Co. Roscommon

Roscommon Historical and Archaeological Society,
Contact address: The Secretary, Castlestrange, Castlecoote P.O., Co. Roscommon.
They publish an annual journal.

Tisrara Heritage Society,
Ms. Eileen Healy, Carrowward, Mount Talbot, Co. Roscommon

County Roscommon Family History Society (CRFHS)
Bealnamullia, Athlone. Co. Roscommon
Email: crfhs@eircom.net   or   rendell@eircom.net
www.geocities.com/Heartland/Pines/7030/
This Society was established in 1993 with the goals:
o   To record and preserve information related to County Roscommon People.

o   To Publish information on, about, and in connection with County Roscommon.

o   To build and maintain a library of such information.

o   To assist researchers and family geneaologists whenever possible within the confines of staff availablity.

Society membership is open and are from many countries. It also publishes an annual journal and back copies are available. The society's Library includes:

Family Records	Emigration data	Marriage records
Birth data	Heraldry	Death data
Family Trees	Convict records	Historical information
Photographs	Register of Names	Foreign records
Church records	Land records	Wills
Census records	Local Publications	
Maps	Graveyard inscriptions	

The Society also publishes results of research undertaken by members. These include:

o   Freeholders of Roscommon, index of Surnames, 1830; 1831 – 1833; 1839.

o   Convictions in Roscommon,1830-1832

o   Births, Deaths & Marriages, 1848-1854 (extracts from newspapers)

o   Births, Deaths & Marriages, 1855-1859 (extracts from newspapers)

o   Kelly Collection, Notes on family of-

o   Roscommon Soldiers who died in World War 1. (Irish Regiments)

o   Roscommon People (Strays from other sources)

The Main Irish Archives:

National Archives of Ireland (NAI)
Bishop Street, Dublin 8
Tel: +353 (0)1 407 2300:   Fax: +353 (0)1 407 2333
Email: mail@nationalarchives.ie
Website: www.nationalarchives.ie

National Library of Ireland (NLI)
Kildare Street, Dublin 2
Tel: +353 (0)1 603 0200:   Fax: +353 (0)1 676 6690
Email: info@nli.ie
Website: www.nli.ie

Registry of Deeds
Henrietta Street, Dublin 1, Ireland Website: www.landregistry.ie
Contact: Anna Gordon, Genealogical Enquiries
Tel: +353 1 804 8412 & Fax: +353 1 804 8406
Email: anna.gordon@landregistry.ie

Dublin City Library and Archives (Pearse Street Library)
138-144 Pearse Street, Dublin 2
Tel: +353 1 674 4999
Email: dublinstudies@dublincity.ie or cityarchives@dublincity.ie
Website: www.dublincity.ie/living_in_the_city/libraries/
Opening Hours Mon to Thurs: 10:00 am – 8:00 pm; Friday, Saturday:
10:00 am – 5:00 pm: Sunday closed

The Genealogical Office
2 Kildare Street, Dublin 2
Tel: +353 1 603 0200 & Fax: +353 1 676 6690 or +353 1 662 1062
Email: info@nli.ie: Website: www.nli.ie
Opening Hours: Monday to Friday, 10:00 am to 12:45 pm and 2:00 pm
to 4:30 pm

General Register Office (GRO)
Convent Road, Roscommon, Co. Roscommon
Tel: +353 (0) 90 6632900 & Fax: +353 (0) 90 6632999
Website: www.groireland.ie

There is also an office and search room at the Dublin Office:
Joyce House, 8-11 Lombard Street East, Dublin 2
Tel: +353 (0)1 671 1000 & Fax: +353 (0)1 671 1243

The Research Room at Joyce House is open from Monday to Friday.
for the purposes of searching the indexes to birth, death, and marriage
records and obtaining photocopies and certificates. Certificates are also
available from any Superintendent Registrar's Office (listed below) on
application in person or by post.

The LDS Family History Centres: There are 3 centres in Ireland located as follows:
- Finglas Road, Dublin 9, Ireland. Website: www.familysearch.org/
- Sarsfield Road, Wilton, Cork, Ireland. Tel: +353 21 489 7050
- Doradoyle Road, Limerick, Co. Limerick, Ireland. Tel: +353 61 309 443

Representative Church Body Library (RCBL)
Braemor Park, Churchtown, Dublin 14
Tel: +353 (0)1 492 3979 & Fax: +353 (0)1 492 4770
Email: library@ireland.anglican.org
Website: www.ireland.anglican.or/library/

Valuation Office
Irish Life Complex, Middle Abbey Street, Dublin 1
Tel: (0)1 817 1045: Email: info@valoff.ie: Website: www.valoff.ie

Genealogical Society of Ireland
Honorary Secretary, 11 Desmond Avenue, Dún Laoghaire, County Dublin
Email: editor@familyhistory.ie
Website: www.familyhistory.ie

The Irish Genealogical Research Society
18 Stafford Avenue, Rainham, Kent ME8 OEP, England
Email: info@igrsoc.org
Website: www.igrsoc.org/

Websites
The Leitrim-Roscommon genealogy website (http://www.leitrim-roscommon.com) provides sources for research in NW Connacht, maps of different administrative divisions, and information on specific families located in the region.
For research on wealthy landed families, (either for information on these families, or to find estate records), a useful website is www.burkes-peerage.net/sites/ireland/sitepages/

Endnotes

1. Donald Lines Jacobus, *Genealogy as Pastime and Profession*, Genealogical Publishing Co., Inc., Baltimore, Maryland, first edition 1930, second edition revised, 1968, page 41

2. Brian Gurrin, "An Examination of the 1749 Census of the Diocese of Elphin,", Marie-Louise Legg, editor, *The Census of Elphin 1749*, IMC, Dublin, 2004, page XXXVii

3. Gurrin, "An Examination of the 1749 Census of the Diocese of Elphin,", *The Census of Elphin 1749*, page XXXVii

4. http://archiver.rootsweb.com/th/read/Ireland/, 19 December 2004

5. Rosemary ffolliott, "Irish Census Returns and Census Substitutes", *Irish Genealogy, A Record Finder*, page 55

6. Margaret Dickson Falley, *Irish and Scotch-Irish Ancestral Research*, Volume I, originally published, 1962, reprinted Genealogical Publishing Co., Baltimore, 1998, page 174.

7. Tony McCarthy, *The Irish Roots Guide*, The Lilliput Press, Dubin, 1991, page 6

8. Gurrin, "An Examination of the 1749 Census of the Diocese of Elphin,", *The Census of Elphin 1749*, page XXXVii

9. Dr. R.S. J. Clarke, "The Value of Tombstone Inscriptions," *The Irish Ancestor,* Vol. 1. No. 1, Dublin, 1959, page 17.

10. Margaret Dickson Falley, *Irish and Scotch Ancestral Research*, Genealogical Publishing Company, Baltimore, Maryland, 1962, fourth printing 1998, Page 417

11. Tony McCarthy, *The Irish Roots Guide*, Lilliput Press, Dublin, 1991, pages 35-36.

12. *Resource Roscommon*. CD-ROM, Part J9...Major landholders in 1876, John Hunter, Brisbane, March 2003

13. Roscommon County Council, 100 years of Local Government, 1899 to 1999. Frank Friel, Herald Printworks, Boyle

14. John Grenham, *Tracing Your Irish Ancestors*, 2nd Edition, Gill & Macmillan, Dublin 1999, page 44.

15. Donal Begley, 'Genealogical Matter in the Publications of the IMC', *Irish Genealogy, A Record Finder*, Heraldic Artists Ltd., Dublin, 1981, page 108.

16. Terence Dooley (MaryAnn Lyons, editor), *Sources for the Landed Estates in Ireland*, Irish Academic Press, Dublin 2000, page 1.

17. Randal MacDonnell, *The Lost Houses of Ireland*, Weidenfield & Nicolson, London, 2002, page 55

18. Brian Smith, *Tracing Your Mayo Ancestors*, Flyleaf Press, Dublin 1997, page 73.

19. Ian Cantwell, Memorials of the Dead Counties Galway & Mayo (Western Seaboard) CD-Rom, Eneclann Dublin 2002

20. R. Andrew Pierce, *The Stones Speak; Irish Place Names from Inscriptions in Boston's Mount Calvary Cemetery*, New England Historic Genealogical Society, Boston, 2000, page 188

21. Sean Murphy, Lecture 7 Notes, *Occupational and Service Records*, 8 March 2004

22. Brenda Howley, "The Arigna Mining Experience," *The Corran Herald*, Ballymote Heritage Group, Issue 38, 2005/2006, pages 58-59

23. Brian Smith, *Tracing Your Mayo Ancestors*, Flyleaf Press, Dublin, 1997, page 39.

24. "From Hedge School to National Board, 1810-1861," Roscommon Historical and Archaeological Society Journal, Volume 1, 1986, pp. 10-13.

25. Same

26. John Grenham, Tracing Your Irish Ancestors, third edition, Gill & Macmillan, Dublin, 2006, page 157

27. Gurrin, "An Examination of the 1749 Census of the Diocese of Elphin,", *The Census of Elphin 1749*, page XXXViii, The only known surviving data for Elphin are the parish aggregate figures for Ahamlish parish in north County Sligo from the 1766 census (NAI, Ms. 2471)

28. Anne Chambers, *At Arm's Length; Aristocrats in the Republic of Ireland*, New Island, Dublin, 2004, page 104

29. Eileen McGowan, "Surnames of County Roscommon," *Irish Roots*, Belgrave Publications, Cork, Issue No. 1, 1993, pp. 20-21

30. Ryan, James G., *Irish Records*, Ancestry and Flyleaf Press, Dublin, 1997, page 473

Index

1641 Rebellion 136
1798 Rebellion 31

A

Abbey Boyle 114, 119, 132
Abby Carthron 66
account books 55, 60, 65
Achrony 16, 78, 84, 87, 90, 117, 122, 139, 141
Acts of Settlement 27
Adamson 130
Administration 6, 83, 84, 86, 87, 88
Administration Bond 83
Administrative Divisions 7, 15, 17
Administrator 83
adventurers 27
Advertiser 96
Aghrim 118
Ahanagh 37
Ailmer 107, 125
Ainsworth 70, 107, 109, 110, 111, 112, 114, 115, 120, 123, 124, 130
Alderford 122
Aldworth 107, 119
Alumni Dublinenses 100, 101
Analecta Hibernica 29, 33, 89, 121 105
Aneenaghara 76
Anglo-Irish landlords 55
Annals of Connacht 105
Annals of Loch Cé, 105
Annesville 110
Ardcarn 19, 20, 33, 42, 67, 68, 73, 75
Ardcarne 37, 42
Ardclare 37, 38
Ardkenna 68
Arigna 45, 75, 94, 131, 132, 139, 150
Army Lists 30
Ash-Hurst 131
Ashford 121, 126
Association for the Preservation of the Memorials of the Dead 79
Athleague 19, 20, 31, 37, 42, 63, 69, 116, 118, 140

Athlone 10, 15, 29, 30, 33, 34, 37, 39, 47, 51, 54, 59, 64, 65, 67, 68, 69, 72, 74, 76, 77, 81, 96, 109, 111, 115, 116, 124, 126, 127, 130, 131, 137, 138, 139, 140, 141, 144
Athlone Corporation 130
Athlone Independent 96
Athlone Sentinel 96
Athlone voters 34
Attorneys 93
Attroy 58
Aughrim 19, 20, 37, 38, 44, 67, 80, 118, 119, 128, 144
Aylward 125, 130

B

Bagot 107, 114
Balfe 54, 57, 107, 108, 110, 117
Ballaghadereen 78
Ballinasloe 42, 110, 123, 138
Ballinderry 117
Ballindrimly 73
Ballinemly 122
Ballinenly 122
Ballinglass 127
Ballinlough 11, 37, 75, 77
Ballinree 59
Ballintemple 80
Ballintober 10, 15, 19, 20, 29, 42, 58, 69, 73, 74, 77
Ballintober, 10, 29, 58, 69, 73, 74, 77
Ballintubber 42, 59, 73, 77, 123, 140
Ballinturly 140
Ballyfarnon 45, 94
Ballyfinegan 110
Ballyfinny 117
Ballyforan 37, 118, 119
Ballygar 37
Ballyglass 68, 77
Ballyhaunis 11
Ballykilcline 33, 135
Ballylyotts 67
Ballymoe 10, 15, 29, 42, 60, 77, 107, 110, 122
Ballymore 74

Ballymot 139
Ballymurray 59, 112, 127
Ballymurry 40, 59, 111
Ballynakill 19, 20
Ballynorm 67
Banada Morris 64
Banns 89
baptisms 16, 35, 39
baptizatus 41
Barnewall 108, 125
Barony 9, 10,15, 17, 18, 51, 64, 65, 68, 69, 73, 76, 109, 110, 122, 123, 127, 138
Barristers 93
Baslick 19, 20, 58, 59, 73, 74, 121
Battlebridge 37, 39
Bealnager 125
Beechwood 116, 130
Beirne 107, 137
Belangare 125, 141
Belcarrow 130
Benson 131
Berington 57, 108
Betham Abstracts 85
Betham manuscripts 85, 89, 90, 105
Bettifield 110
Bettyville 110
Bever 112
Beytagh 76
Bingham 108, 127
Births 8, 23, 145
Blackburn 108
Bogginfin 115
Bohagh 63
Bond 57, 83, 90, 108
bonds 70, 71, 87, 90
Books of Survey and Distribution 26, 27, 104
Boswell 30, 57, 108, 130
Boyce 108
Boyle 10, 11, 15, 19, 20, 29, 31, 33, 37, 43, 46, 54, 62, 66, 67, 68, 69, 73, 74, 75, 76, 77, 91, 93, 96, 97, 108, 109, 114, 117, 119, 123, 125, 126, 127, 131, 132, 136, 138, 140, 141, 143, 149
Boyle Gazette 96

Brabazon 109
Bracloon Castle 112
Brennan 76, 107
Brett 109
Brewery 77
Briarfield 116
Brideswell Town 50
British Isles Vital Records Index 8, 24
British Museum 27, 67, 72, 110, 124
Browne 57, 58
Brownrigg 77
Bruen 58, 94, 109
Buckfield 74, 119
Bucknall 58
Bucknall, Charles 58
Bulgaria 125
Bumlin 19, 20, 37, 39, 45, 71, 80, 124
Burgess, Rev. J.B. 33, 39
burgesses 75
burial 35, 39, 40, 41, 79, 80
Burke 109
Burne 140
Butler 109, 118
Byrne 29, 30, 109, 123, 137

C

Caldwell 110
Calendars of Wills 88
Callow 64, 69
Cam 19, 20, 45, 58,80, 81, 109, 139
Camagh 122
Cambo 111, 118
Cambo Castle 111
Camma 19, 20, 45
Cancelled Land Books 49, 50
Canterbury, Court of 86
Capel 110
Carbally 110
Carnaglass 58
Carnamadda 59
Carranure 107
Carrick-on-Shannon 33, 73, 96, 144
Carrickmaine 130
Carrig 122
Carrigan Beg 61
Carrigan More 61

Carroanaskagh 57
Carrongier 115
Carrowcrin 63, 64
Carrowgarve 68
Carrowkeel 63
Carrowntemple 81
Carrowreagh 123
Carson 58, 59, 110
Carson, John 58, 59, 110
Cartrona 127
Cartrons Lodge 114
Carunemore 67
Castle Coote 127
Castlecoote 99, 144
Castlegar 67
Castle McDermott 122
Castlemeaghan 117
Castlemore 19, 20, 43, 117
Castleplunkett 127
Castlerea 62, 73, 74, 77, 78, 91, 93, 128, 132, 140
Castlereagh 10, 15, 54, 60, 63, 73, 76, 77
Castle Ruby, 111
Castlestrange 120, 144
Castleteheen 58, 68
Castletown Papers 58, 59
Catholic 8, 9, 16, 23, 33, 35, 40, 41, 42, 80, 93, 100, 138, 141
Caulfield 58, 60, 63, 110, 115
cavalry 31, 62
Cavetown 122, 123
CELT Project 105
Census 7, 9, 27, 28, 29, 30, 31, 32, 33, 34, 35, 93, 104, 138, 140, 144, 145, 149, 150
Census of Ireland circa 1659 29
Certificate 6, 11, 119, 123
Chamney, Anne 29
Chancery Inquisitions 88
Charles II 27
Charlestown 119, 120
Cherryfield 68
Chichester 108, 110, 136
Chiefs 27, 105, 118
Choppyne 120
Chronicle 96

Churchboro 77
Church of Ireland 8, 16, 17, 29, 35, 36, 37, 39, 40, 51, 79, 80, 84, 89, 93, 100
Church of Jesus Christ of Latter Day Saints 8, 24, 36
Church Records 7, 35, 36, 40, 42, 141, 144
Civil Divisions 15
Civil Parish 16, 41, 42, 48
Civil Records 144
Civil Registration 7, 23
Civil Survey 1654 104
Clare, Fr. Wallace 29
Clarke 78, 138, 149
Cleaver 58
clergy 91, 93, 100
Clery 105
Clonalis 54, 56, 104, 125, 140
Clonarke 124
Clonbigney 123
Clonbrock 31, 58, 59, 60, 112, 113
Clonbrock Estate 31
Clonee 76
Clonerigh 126
Clonfert, 16, 84, 87, 90
Clonnyn 123
Clonsilla 111
Cloonagloshy 57
Cloonbigny 123
Cloonbonny 112
Clooncraff 19, 20
Clooner Blakeny 115
Cloonfinlogh 57, 58
Cloonfinlough 19, 20, 45, 65, 71, 80
Cloonlaughnan 64
Cloonshanvoyle, 112
Cloontuskert 19, 20, 43, 80
Cloonygormican 19, 20
Cloonyquin 73
clothiers 91
Commercial directories 91, 93
Commough 65
Compossicion Booke 27
Compton 110
Connaught Ranger 98
Connolly 58, 138

Connor 107, 114, 117, 118, 124, 125, 140, 141
Conolly 110
Conolly Papers 110
Conroy 109, 110, 126
Consistorial Court 84
Convert Rolls 29, 30
Coolavin 11, 104, 105, 122
Coolougher 122
Coote 54, 59, 127
Corbally 59, 74
Corderry 69
Cordrumman 68
Cormick 110, 111
Cormick Papers 110
Corradrehid, 72
Correal Valley 140
Corregard House 127
Corron 65
Cotes 78
Cranagh 117
Creagh 19, 20, 42, 109
Creeve 19, 20, 43, 62, 64, 67
Cregg 34, 111
Crofton Estate 30, 33, 59
Croghan 37, 121
Crohan 54, 110, 121
Cromwell 27, 29
Crosbie 60, 111, 129
Cruice 111
Cryan 11
Culeenbag 59
Currihina 108
Curry 65
Cusack 111, 112

D

D'Alton, John 61, 112
Dalton 60, 63, 138
Dawson, Walter 62
Dease 107
Deaths 22, 23, 145
deeds 33, 52, 53, 57, 69, 70, 71, 74, 78, 88, 111, 116, 127, 132
de Exeter 114
De Freyne 54, 60, 63, 114, 115, 122

Denning 64, 75
Derham Lodge 128
Derrylahan 63
Derrysra 99
Devanny 112
Dillon 31, 54, 58, 61, 62, 63, 111, 112, 113, 116, 122
Diocesan court 78, 84, 87, 89, 90, 140, 141, 144
Diocese 16, 35, 36, 37, 40, 41, 42, 78, 87, 88, 90, 117, 124, 137, 139, 140, 141, 149, 150
Diocese of Tuam 40, 41, 88
Directories 7, 91, 93, 94, 144
disestablishment 84
Dobbyn 107
Dodwell 77, 113, 115
Dolling 62
Domvile 62, 75
Donamon 38, 110
Donnellan 112, 113
Dowling 113, 121, 129
Drimdoe 66
Dromahair 65
Dromshare 114
Drum 19, 20, 38, 39, 47, 124, 138
Drumatemple 19, 42
Drumdoe 126
Drumsna 114, 121
Drury 109, 113
Dublin City Library 6, 24, 146
Duckworth 62, 113
Dunamon 19, 20, 44
Dundas 31, 62, 113
Dundas Estate 31
Dundermott 125
Dungannon 72
Dungar 114
Dunne 113, 114
Dysart 19, 20, 39, 43, 80, 109

E

Earls of Essex 110
Eastersnow 19, 20, 38
Eccles 130
ecclesiastical 11, 16, 93, 135

Ecclesiastical Divisions 16
Education 6, 100
Egan 73, 75, 138
elections 31, 70, 72, 75, 135
Electoral Divisions 16, 17
Ellis Island records 135
Elm Park 127
Elphin 9, 16, 19, 20, 28, 30, 35, 36,
    38, 43, 54, 64, 66, 67, 71, 74,
    80, 84, 87, 90, 91, 93, 104, 110,
    116, 119, 120, 121, 124, 125,
    128, 137, 140, 144, 149, 150
Emigrants 33, 135
emigration 9, 70, 135
Emlagh 76, 77
Emlaghbeg 110
Emla 74
Encumbered Estates 52
Eneclann 31, 49, 82, 88, 89, 93, 104,
    136, 138, 139, 150
Ennfield 114
Erwin 62, 64
Established Church 79, 89
estates 7, 52, 54, 55, 56, 57, 58, 59,
    60, 61, 62, 63, 64, 65, 66, 67,
    69, 73, 74, 75, 76, 77, 108, 110,
    111, 115, 128, 130, 135
Estersnow 19, 20, 31, 45, 59, 62, 67
Eustace, P.B. 86, 87
Evans 57, 62
evictions 33, 55, 76
Executor: 83

F

Falkiner, Rev. R 78
Fallon 107, 114, 117, 118, 138
Family Histories 7, 107
Famine 9, 139, 140
farmers 55, 91, 93
Fernhall 117
fever 70, 131
Field Books 49, 76
Field Name Books 17
First World War 93
Fitzgibbon 63
Fitzmaurice 63, 64

Fitzsimons 114
Flanagan 107, 114, 126, 132, 135
Flattery 131
Flynn 94, 107
Folliot 114
Folliott 110
Fort William 131
Four Masters 105
Four Mile House 127
Fox 65, 114, 120
Freeholder's Lists 144
freeholders 31 67, 68, 69, 72, 145
French 54, 58, 60, 63, 73, 114, 115,
    119, 122, 123, 138
Frenchlawn 114
Frenchpark 10, 15, 44, 46, 54, 60, 63,
    67, 76, 77, 114
Frizell 59, 73
Fry 115
Frybrook 115
Fuerty 19, 20, 31, 38, 42, 63, 69, 80,
    116

G

Gallach 118
Galway Express 96
Game Certificates 33
Gately 81
Gaynor 115
Gazette 96
Gazetteer 17
Gearty 34, 115
Genealogical Office 8, 89, 133, 139,
    146
Genealogical Society of Ireland 147
Genealogies 7, 103, 105
General Register Office 8, 23, 24, 146
Gethin 63, 115
Gethin Papers 115
Gillstown 124, 128, 129
Glanballythomas 54, 57, 108
Glancey 63
Glancy 63
Glancy, Mary 63
Glans 57, 108
Glass 115

Glens 108
Goff 54, 110, 115
Gordon 63, 146
Gore 115, 116, 127
Grace 116
Graham 116
Grange 69, 111, 121
Grantors Indexes 52
gravestones 7, 79
Greene 112, 116
Grehan 116
Greville 63
Greyfield 125
Griffith's Valuation 34, 49, 56, 139, 144
GRO 8, 22, 23, 24, 25, 36, 146
grocers 91
Gunning 31, 63
Gunning Estate 31
Gurrin, Brian 30

H

Hampton 76
Hamrock 3, 4, 5, 6, 11, 22, 51
Handcock 63, 65, 130
Handran, George 17
Hanly 57, 58, 60, 61, 63, 64, 74
Harleian Charter 110
Harman 63, 64, 65, 116, 119, 120, 128, 129
Harrington Papers 135
Harris 64
Harristown 132
Hart, Robert 58
Hartland 67, 68, 71, 122, 123
Hartstrong 120
Hatch 116, 127
Hatley Manor 64, 73
Hawkes 116
Hayes, Richard 56, 103
Hearth Money Rolls 104
Heathfield 108
hedge schools 99
Henry 67, 68, 71, 73, 78, 108, 109, 110, 112, 113, 115, 116, 119, 120, 123, 128, 130

Heppenstall 116
Herald and Western Adviser 98
Heritage Books 41
Herlihy, Jim 94
Hertfordshire Record 110
Heywood 75
Higgins 62, 73, 81, 107
High Lake 114, 115
High Park 75
Hodson 63, 64, 116
Hodson's bay 116
Hoey 64, 75
Hogan, Garret 65
Homses, Joseph A. 60
House Books 49
householders 30
House of Lords 104, 109, 123
Houston 116
Hughes 64, 116, 132
Hughestown 124
Huguenots 27
Hussey 56, 116, 117, 124, 130
Hussey de Burgh, O.H. 56
Hyde 64, 117
Hynde 117

I

Ikearon 58
Immediate Lessor 56
Index of Surnames 49, 51
Inscriptions 7, 79, 80, 81, 149, 150
Intestate 83
Ireland 4, 5, 6, 8, 9, 11, 15, 16, 17, 21, 23, 24, 25, 29, 32, 33, 35, 36, 37, 39, 40, 49, 51, 55, 56, 62, 66, 70, 79, 80, 81, 84, 85, 86, 88, 89, 91, 93, 94, 95, 99, 100, 103, 104, 105, 107, 110, 113, 117, 120, 125, 133, 135, 136, 138, 139, 140, 142, 143, 145, 146, 147, 149, 150
Irish Ancestor 8, 87, 149
Irish Archaeological Society 105, 141
Irish Architectural Archive 58, 59
Irish Army List 61
Irish Catholic Directory 40

Irish Connection 137
Irish Constabulary 94
Irish Family History Foundation 8, 143
Irish Folklore Commission 100, 143
Irish Genealogical Research Society 8, 140, 147
Irish Genealogist 109, 110, 113, 117, 120, 123, 127, 140
Irishman 96
Irish Manuscripts Commission 8, 26, 28, 55
Irish Roots 11, 121, 140, 149, 150
Irwin 64, 67, 108, 117
Ivernoon 19, 20

J

Jacobites 29
Jebb 117
John Rylands Library 78, 125, 126
Johnson 64
Johnston 69, 76, 117
Jones 66, 117, 135

K

Kane 75
Keane, E. 93
Keane, Edward 57
Kearney 78
Keelbanada 64
Keelogues, 118
Keenagh 118, 119
Kelly 25, 34, 40, 66, 70, 78, 107, 114, 117, 118, 119, 121, 124, 125, 126, 127, 128, 130, 141, 145
Kelly, Fiagh 66, 121
Kellybrook 118
Kenney 119
Kenny 107, 114
Keogh 64, 136, 143
Keogh, John 136, 143
Keon 64
Kilbride 19, 20, 39, 44, 99
Kilbryan 19, 20, 38, 59, 67
Kilcash 118
Kilcoffin 38

Kilcolagh 19, 20
Kilcolman 19, 20, 43
Kilcooley 31, 63
Kilcooly 19, 20, 68
Kilcorkey 19, 20, 38, 44
Kilcorky 58
Kildare Place Society 100
Kileglass 119
Kilgeffin 38
Kilgefin 19, 20, 59, 71
Kilglass 19, 20, 33, 38, 44, 47, 71, 135, 138
Kilkeevan 19, 38, 44, 73
Killahan 118, 126
Killala 78, 87, 90, 139
Killcolman 117
Killenvoy 19, 20, 38, 39
Killinvoy 19, 20, 47, 59
Killmoves 117
Killnamannagh 64
Killtee 129
Killukin 19, 20, 38, 46, 68, 73
Killumod 19, 20, 38, 46, 59, 68, 73
Killumod. 68, 73
Kilmacumpsy 72
Kilmacumsy 19, 20
Kilmeane 19, 20, 59
Kilmore 19, 20, 38, 44, 64, 87, 90, 121, 125, 127, 132, 140, 141, 144
Kilnamanagh 19, 20, 31, 45, 62, 67, 71
Kilnamona 68
Kilronan 19, 20, 30, 33, 39, 45, 57, 74, 75, 77, 120, 122
Kiltee 121
Kilteevan 19, 20, 47, 80
Kiltimaine 77
Kiltobranks 77
Kiltoom 19, 20, 39, 45, 48, 139
Kiltrustan 19, 20, 45, 59, 71, 80
Kiltullagh 19, 20, 39, 45, 73
Kiltulogue 58
Kilverdin 80
King 54, 61, 63, 64, 65, 74, 81, 93, 109, 114, 116, 119, 120, 121, 123, 124, 128, 129

King's Inns 93, 109, 123
King James 61
Kingsborough 131
Kingsland 109, 113
Kingston 64, 65, 110, 119, 120
Kirkwood 120
Knockadoe 120
Knocknagauna 77
Knott 120
Knox 65, 67, 72, 139

L

L'Estrange 121
labourers 64, 71, 132
Lambert 120
Land Commission 53, 56, 57, 60, 75, 89
Landed Gentry 56
Land Index 52
Land League 75, 76
Landlord 56
Landowners 56
Land Records 7, 31, 34, 49, 144
Land Registry 53
Lane 65, 114, 120, 121
La Touche, 94
Latter Day Saints 8, 24, 36
Lawder 121
lawyers 91
Layden 94
LDS Family History Centres 147
lease books 55, 67
le Botiller 109
Leech 75
Leeds Public Libraries 65
Leheny 94
Leigarr 122
Leimgarr 121
Leitrim Journal 96
Lewis 17, 66, 142
Leybeg 117
Lillie 66
Linea Antiqua 105
linen industry 71
Lion 66, 121
Lisalway 62
Lisboy 76, 77

Liscloghan 127
Lisdorne 54, 111
Lisgarve 63
Lisliddy 76, 77
Lissadurn 54, 66
Lissayegan 110
Lissonuffy 19, 20, 45, 80
Lissyallen 58
Listhomasroe 63
Lloyd 54, 66, 94, 107, 110, 111, 121
Loan Society Accounts 34
Longfield 67, 69, 76, 77, 121
Longford, 9, 65, 69, 71, 73, 75, 108, 111, 118, 126, 132, 138, 140
Longworth 67, 130
Lorton 65, 67
Lough Gara 9, 76
Loughglin 31, 61, 62
Loughglinn 39, 54
Low Park 117, 129
Lucy 67, 129
Ludlow 115
Lugboy 123
Lynam, P.J. 78
Lynch 94, 113, 121, 123
Lynn 94
Lyster 121, 131

M

MacCormack 121
MacDermott 121, 122
MacLysaght 13, 25, 103, 107, 121
MacManaway 122
Magennis 122
Maher 78
Mahon 33, 54, 64, 67, 68, 69, 70, 71, 72, 73, 122, 123, 127, 135, 136
Malthouse Park, 73
Manners 68, 73
Mantua 116
Manuscript Sources 56, 75, 103, 133, 139, 140
maps 17, 19, 21, 34, 50, 55, 58, 59, 60, 61, 62, 63, 64, 65, 66, 67, 68, 69, 72, 73, 74, 75, 76, 77, 78, 128, 130, 145, 147

Mapother 123
Markby, Alfred 62
Marksmen 33
Marriages 7, 8, 16, 23, 24, 25, 35, 36,
    37, 39, 40, 41, 42, 83, 86, 87,
    89, 90, 94, 114, 129, 145
Marriage Licences 86, 89, 90
Martinstown, 112
Mason 123
matrimonium 41
Mayo 9, 11, 15, 27, 51, 75, 76, 78, 88,
    96, 98, 111, 112, 113, 116, 117,
    123, 130, 136, 141, 150
McAnlis 133, 139
McCausland 67
McDermott 68, 107, 121, 122
McDermotts 94
McDonagh 107
McDonogh 111, 122
McGan 122
McKeogh 112, 122
McTiernan 94
medical 91, 93
memorial records 79
Methodist 35, 40
Midland Telegraph 96
military 11, 91
Militia 30, 63, 93
Millers 94
Mills 94
Milton 125
Miltown 74
mines 94, 131, 132
Missing Friends 135
Moher 58
Moland 68
Moneymore 59
Montgomery 123
Moore 19, 20, 33, 39, 46, 117, 121,
    123, 126, 128, 142
Moore & Drum 39
Moran 29, 76, 78, 135, 140, 143
Moran, Malachy 29, 76, 78, 135
Moran Manuscripts 143
More-O'Ferral 121
Morgan 81

Morley 109, 123
mortgages 53, 57
Mote Park 54, 59, 100
Mount Allen 94
Mount Druid 125
Mount Erris 113
Mount Plunkett 116, 118
Mountrath 68, 115
Mount Talbot 81, 129, 144
Moycarn 10, 15, 29, 63, 76, 77
Moycarnon 121, 129
Moylurg 122, 139, 140
Moyne 57, 58
Moyvannan 62
Mulhall 123
Mullaghmore 118
Mullagnashee 77
Mullally 126
Mullen 54, 69
Mulligan 68
Mulloy 124, 126
Mullymux 74
Mulvihill 65
Muncaster Mss 116
Murphy 6, 54, 69, 84, 150
Murray 74, 107
Muschamp 120, 123, 128

N

Naghten: 124, 126
National Archives 6, 8, 82, 138, 145
National Library of Ireland 6, 8, 25,
    146
National Schools 100
Naughten 124, 126
Newcoman 120, 124
New England Historic and Genealogi-
    cal Society 81
New Park 121
Newspapers 7, 95
Newsplan 95
Noone 94
Nugent 69, 124
NUI Galway 58, 59
Nymphsfield 126

O

O'Brien, M.S. 105
O'Byrne, Eileen 29, 30
O'Caiside 124
O'Casey 124
O'Connell 124
O'Connor 114, 117, 118, 124, 125, 140, 141
O'Connors 94, 140
O'Conors 56
O'Donell 125
O'Donnellans 125
O'Donovan, John 78, 105, 131
O'Fallon 114
O'Farrell 123, 125
O'Hara 105, 126, 130
O'Hart's Irish Pedigrees 102
O'Kelly 117, 118, 119, 126, 141
O'Loghlen 114, 126, 132
O'Loghlen Papers 126, 132
O'Loughlin 122
O'Mulconry 110, 126
O'Mulloy 124, 126
O'Naghten 124, 126
O'Reilly 69, 123, 126
O'Reillys 94
O'Rorke 69
O'Rourke 126, 127
Oakes 124
Oak Park, 109, 114
Oak Port 124
Oakport 54, 115, 124
occupation 23, 34, 86, 88, 89, 94
Occupational 7, 91, 150
officers 31, 62, 93
O Gara 105
Ogulla 19, 20, 46, 59
Old Athlone Society 137, 140
O Maolalla 126
Oran 19, 20, 39, 46, 117
Ordnance Survey 17, 21, 50, 65, 76, 78, 141
Ormsby 69, 108, 117, 127, 132
Orwark 126
Oughteriry 124
outlawed 29

Owen 66, 72, 116, 125, 132
Owen Gallagher 72

P

Packenham 123, 127, 131
Pakenham-Mahon 33, 67, 70, 72, 135, 136
Palace Elphin 125
Palmer 115, 116, 127
Palmer Papers 115
Parliamentary Gazetteer 17
Parliamentary Papers 9, 33
pedigree chart/sheet 12, 13
Penal Times 29, 137
Pender, Séamus 29, 105
Pender's 1659 Census 104
Pender's Census 29
Pension Claim Forms 34
Petty, Sir William 29
Pierce, Andrew 81, 150
Pigot 91
Plunkett 29, 111, 115, 116, 118, 122, 126, 127, 140
police 91, 93, 94
Polling Books 29, 31
Pomfret 55
Poor Law Unions 8, 16, 17, 24
Poor Rate 49
Potts 54, 127
Prerogative Administration 86
Prerogative Court: 85
Prerogative Marriage Licence Bonds 90
Prerogative Wills 85, 86, 88, 89, 139
Presbyterian 35, 40, 93
Priests 137, 138
Primary Valuations 49, 50
PRO 8, 27, 36, 93, 94
Probate 17, 83, 84, 86, 127
Protestant 27, 35, 99
Province 15
Public Records Office 83

Q

Quaker 35, 40, 80
Quinn 107

R

Radigan 127
Rahara 19, 20, 65, 109
Raines 115
Rapheak 121, 129
Rathconnelly 57
Rathmile 113, 130
Rathmore 127
Rathmoyle 117
Rebellion Papers 136
rebels 31
Regan 107
Registration Districts 24
Registry of Deeds 6, 49, 52, 86, 87, 146
Reheely 54, 69
rentals 55, 60, 62, 63, 64, 67, 68, 69, 71, 72, 73, 74, 75, 94, 130, 131
Rent roll 59, 68, 69, 74
Representative Church Body Library 6, 8, 36, 147
Reynolds 78, 120, 136
RIC Indices 144
Ridge 67
Roberts 72
Robert White Papers 94, 131
Robinson 130
Rochfort 130
Rockingham 54, 74, 119, 128, 129
Rooskey Bridge 78
Roscommon and Leitrim Gazette 96
Roscommon Champion 97, 98
Roscommon Constitutionalist 97
Roscommon County Library 6, 8, 11, 51, 95, 100, 143
Roscommon Herald 97, 140
Roscommon Heritage and Genealogy Company 8, 143
Roscommon Historical and Archaeological Society 8, 40, 137, 144, 150
Roscommon Journal 97, 98
Roscommon Loan Society 97
Roscommon Messenger 98
Roscommon Reporter 98
Roscommon Town 14, 138, 143

Roscommon Weekly Messenger 98
Ross 63, 67, 71, 72
Rossleven 112
Roxborough 117
Royal Irish Academy 6, 8, 105
Royal Irish Constabulary 94
Runnabacken 75
Runnimead 107
Runnimede 57, 108
Rush Hill 112
Ruskey 138
Rylands, John 78, 125, 126

S

Sallymount 74
Sandford 54, 70, 71, 73, 74, 77, 128, 132
Sandys 128
Sanford 68, 70, 73, 74, 123
Sankey 118, 128
sepultus 41
servants 30
Shadwell, J. 67
Shankill 19, 20, 67, 71, 130
Sheepwalk 122
Shields 112
shoemakers 91
Shragh 63
Sidley, Sir Ralph 116
Simington, R.C. 27, 29
Simpson 128
Skekyn 116
Sketch Pedigrees 85
Skreen 119
Slacke 128
Slata 138
Slater 91, 93
Sliabh Lugha 139
Smith 4, 128, 136, 139, 141, 150
Social directories 91
Society of Friends 40
Society of Genealogists 85, 88
solicitors 55, 56, 76, 107
Spelling 25
Spencer 4, 123, 128
Spinning Wheel Premium 31

Springlaun 113
St. George 58, 72, 73, 111, 121, 128, 132
St. Helena Lodge 130
St. John 19, 20, 39, 47, 116
St. John's 19, 20, 47, 116
St. Peter 19, 20, 37, 39, 47, 81
St. Peter's 19, 20, 37, 47, 81
Stacpoole Kenny Papers 114
Stafford 74, 76, 104, 119, 120, 128, 129, 147
Stafford-King 74, 129
Stafford's Inquisition 104
Stafford Survey 76
Stanley 129, 132
Stapleton Papers 107
Stationery Office 27, 29, 140
Staunton 129
Stowe Collection 69, 78
Stratford 131
Strickland, Charles 62
Strokestown 39, 45, 54, 67, 68, 69, 70, 71, 72, 75, 81, 91, 93, 98, 99, 119, 122, 123, 128, 135, 143
Strokestown Democrat 98
Sunfield 114
Sunnerhill 111
Surnames 7, 49, 51, 87, 103, 104, 107, 133, 140, 145, 150
Sweeney 67, 68

T

Taghboy 19, 20, 81
Taghmaconnell 19, 20, 47, 81
Talbot 60, 81, 111, 127, 129, 144
Talbot-Crosbie 60
Tangier House 126
Tarmon 77, 122
Tarmonbarry 39
Taughboy 39, 69, 74
Taughmaconnell 19, 31, 47, 58, 81, 141
Taylor & Skinner 21
teachers 91, 93, 99, 100
tenant-farmers 55
tenant farmers 55, 91

tenants 27, 30, 31, 52, 55, 56, 57, 58, 59, 60, 62, 63, 64, 65, 67, 68, 69, 71, 72, 73, 74, 76
tenants' lists 55
Tenison 33, 54, 74, 75, 94, 110, 120, 130
Tenison Estate 33
Tenure Books 49
Termonbarry 19, 20, 67, 72
Tessaragh 39
Testamentary Card Index 88
testamentary records 82, 83
The Land Commission 53
Thom's 93, 148
Thomastown 124, 126
Thrift Abstracts 31, 33, 34
Tibohine 19, 20, 39, 46, 47, 73, 122
Tintagh, 66
Tireragh 65
Tirerrill 65
Tisrara 19, 20, 81, 109, 137, 144
Tithe Applotments 31, 49, 50, 51, 78, 136, 144
titulados 29
Toberpatrick 110
Tobervaddy 127
Toler 130
Tollaghane 113
Tonroe 68
Toomna 37, 39
Toomona 111
Toomore 77
Topographical Dictionary 17, 142
Torner 75
Tottenham 75, 108, 130
Toureagh 77
Towey 107
Townshend 132
Trade Directories 144
tradesmen 72, 91
Transplantation 29, 104
Trant 130
Trench 75, 126, 130
Trimlestown 75
Trinity College 8, 57, 100, 101, 128, 136

Tuam 16, 17, 36, 40, 41, 78, 84, 87,
    88, 98, 138, 139
Tuam Herald 98
Tullon 110
Tullyquarter 123
Tulsk 46, 65, 120, 121
Tumna 19, 20, 31, 33, 42, 59, 62
Twomore 77, 113
Tycooly 118

U

University College Dublin 6, 8, 11

V

Valuation Office 6, 49, 50, 147
Vestry minutes 39
Vicars, Sir Arthur 86, 89, 139
Voters 33, 144

W

Walker 62, 130
Wallace Clare 29, 88
Walsh 5, 6, 116, 117, 127, 130, 131
Walshe 130, 131
West 29, 112, 113, 121, 130, 131, 140
Westby 75
Western Impartial Reporter 98
Western Nationalist 98
Weston 118, 131
White 75, 94, 131, 132
Whyte 75, 131
Will Abstracts 84, 89
William Smith O'Brien Petition 136,
    139
Wills 7, 16, 17, 53, 57, 70, 71, 78, 75,
    83, 84, 85, 86, 87, 88, 89, 90,
    128, 129, 132, 139, 141, 145,
    108, 109, 110, 116, 117, 118s,
Willsgrove 54, 63, 75, 110, 132
Windis 115
Woodbrook 120, 124
Woodpark House 124
workers 91
Workhouse 33, 140

Woulfe 13, 103, 104, 114, 126, 132
Woulfe, Rev. Patrick 103
Writeson 115
Wynne 94, 110, 116, 132

Y

Yearly Calendars 88
yeomanry 70